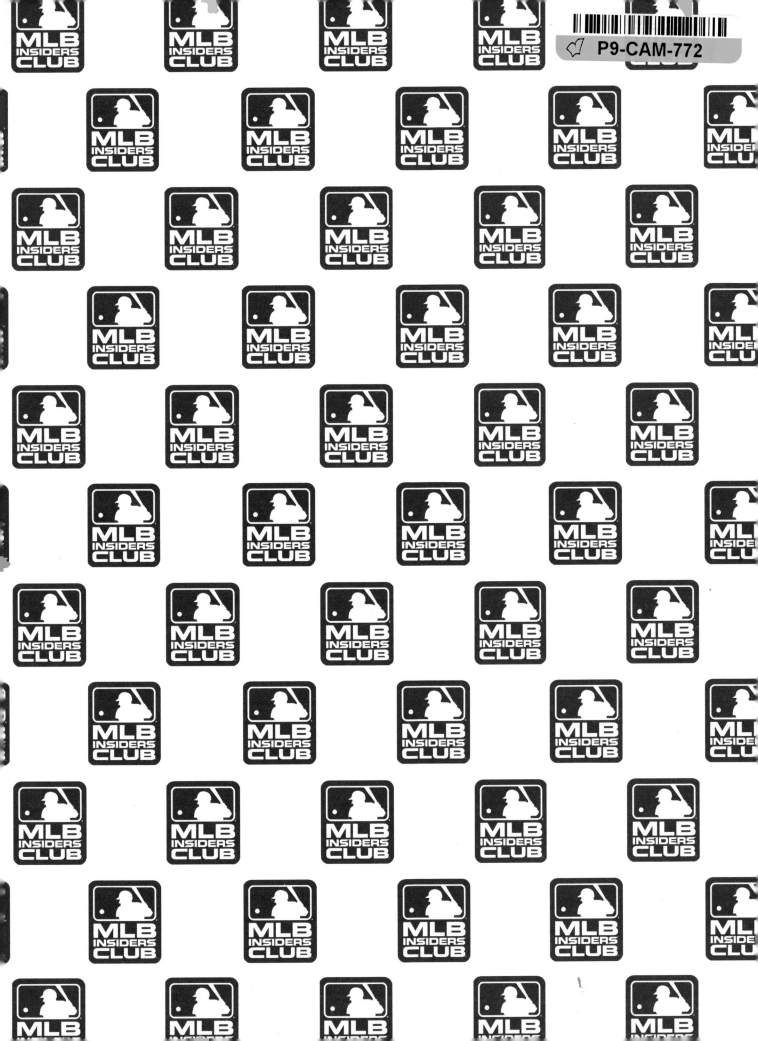

# BASEBALL'S
# GREATEST
# PERSONALITIES

Charming oddballs, dashing rogues and the most
unforgettable characters in Big League history.

**Baseball Insiders Library**™

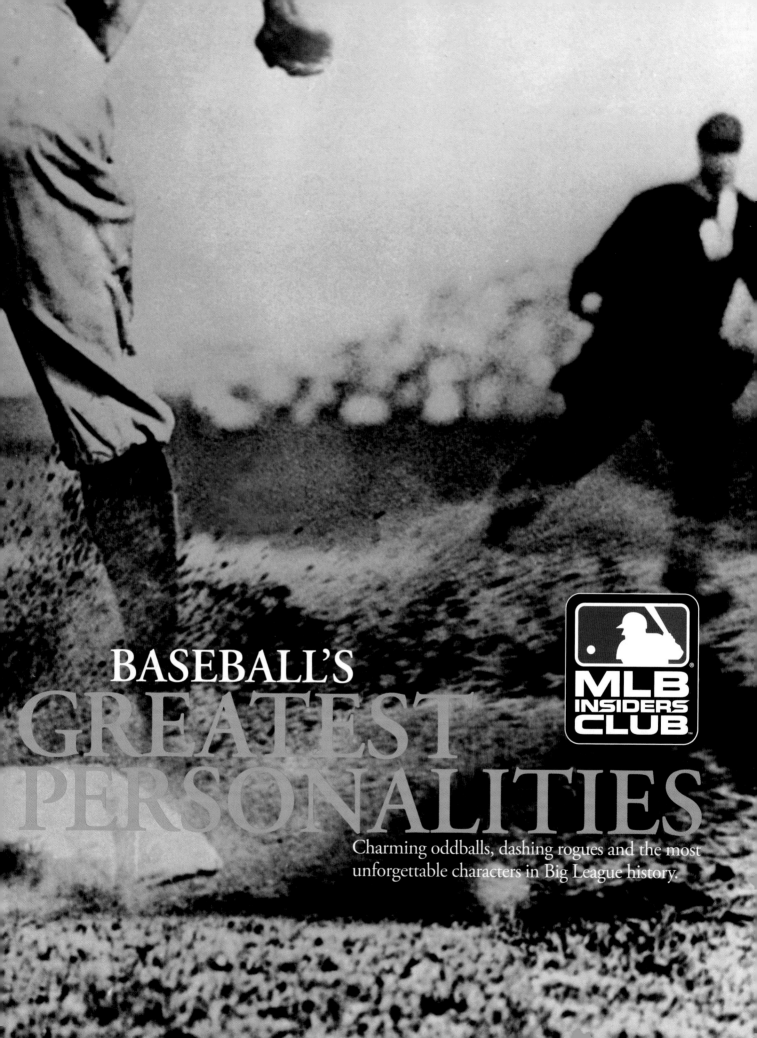

# BASEBALL'S
# GREATEST
# PERSONALITIES

Charming oddballs, dashing rogues and the most
unforgettable characters in Big League history.

# BASEBALL'S GREATEST PERSONALITIES by Troy E. Renck

*Charming oddballs, dashing rogues and the most unforgettable characters in Big League history.*

Printed in 2010

## About the Author

*Troy E. Renck has covered Major League Baseball and the Colorado Rockies since 1996. He has been at the* Denver Post *since 2002, and has served as the national and beat writer since 2006. Renck is also a regular contributior on ESPN's "First Take" Doubleheader segment. He lives in Longmont, Colo., with his wife and two sons.*

## Acknowledgements

Major League Baseball would like to thank Pat Kelly and Milo Stewart Jr. at the National Baseball Hall of Fame and Museum for their invaluable assistance; as well as Bill Francis, Eric Enders and Kristin Nieto for their diligent work in helping to prepare the book for publication.

## Major League Baseball Properties

**Vice President, Publishing**
Donald S. Hintze

**Editorial Director**
Mike McCormick

**Publications Art Director**
Faith M. Rittenberg

**Senior Production Manager**
Claire Walsh

**Associate Editor**
Jon Schwartz

**Associate Art Director**
Melanie Finnern

**Senior Publishing Coordinator**
Anamika Chakrabarty

**Project Assistant Editors**
Chris Greenberg, Jodie Jordan, Jake Schwartzstein

**Editorial Intern**
Allison Duffy

### Major League Baseball Photos

**Director**
Rich Pilling

**Photo Editor**
Jessica Foster

## MLB Insiders Club

**Creative Director**
Tom Carpenter

**Managing Editor**
Jen Weaverling

**Prepress**
Wendy Holdman

2 3 4 5 6 7 8 9 10/15 14 13 12 11 10

Copyright © MLB Insiders Club 2010

ISBN: 978-1-58159-470-6

MLB Insiders Club
12301 Whitewater Drive
Minnetonka, MN 55343

# TABLE OF CONTENTS

# INTRO

In July 1965, the Mets organized Old-Timers Day to fall near skipper Casey Stengel's 75th birthday. When his No. 37 was retired by the fledgling club later in the season and displayed in a glass case, Stengel, ever the deadpan cut-up, told New York fans, "I hope they don't put a mummy in that case."

Stengel, known as the "Ol' Perfessor" after his distinguished and jocular 25-year managerial career which included seven titles in the Bronx, was one of baseball's most fabled characters, a man who could make people pause with a quip or even just his presence.

Yet he is hardly alone among characters of the game. There was a Bird, Mark Fidrych, whose conversations with the baseball

and groundskeeping on the mound electrified Detroit in 1976. There was a clown prince, Max Patkin, who made people giggle in every outpost that had a diamond and a sense of humor. There was a Spaceman, Bill Lee, who spoke out on political issues and dared to call his manager a gerbil. There was even a moon man, Steve Lyons, whose accidental striptease after sliding into first base surprised everyone — including himself. And there was the Babe, whose appetite and largesse on and off the field remains the stuff of legend nearly a century after his career began.

Baseball has certainly introduced fans to some of our culture's most colorful and unforgettable personalities. Some players just

loved to perform sophomoric pranks, believing that a loose clubhouse was a better clubhouse. Tug McGraw ordered takeout to the bullpen, and Jay Johnstone hung Manager Tommy Lasorda's dress pants from a flagpole during Spring Training. Others mastered intimidation, like Bob Gibson and Goose Gossage, frightening opponents with cold-blooded stares.

Some inspired us with their courage and vision. Jackie Robinson broke baseball's color barrier, providing inspiration to everyone in the Negro Leagues. John Montgomery Ward fought for players' rights long before a union was even a figment in anyone's imagination. And some of the most memorable characters became beloved *off* the field, producing the sounds of the game. Their voices became our eyes, making us smile, even if unintentionally, as Phil Rizzuto and Jerry Coleman so often did.

Baseball is a grind, starting in February and running through October, so any and all levity is welcome. Whether hustling in front of adoring hometown fans, lightening the clubhouse mood during a tense pennant race, or using outlandish behavior to test the patience of a front office, the familiar oddballs and passionate grinders bring drama to the baseball season. This rare breed has made us stand up to cheer — and often laugh — enlivening the game and providing memories for generations of fans.

## CHAPTER 1

# RIGHT OF CENTER

*Some Big Leaguers don't just march to the beat of a different drummer; they are propelled by an entirely separate orchestra. Welcome to the wacky world of right-handed pitchers. They can be eccentric and electric, like Detroit's one-hit wonder Mark Fidrych, who gave goosebumps to Motor City fans with each appearance. They can be unique in personality and delivery: Luis Tiant turned his back on hitters during his motion; Dan Quisenberry threw submarine style. Some are just talented goofs, like the incomparable Dizzy Dean. There is even a doctor in the house — tireless reliever Mike Marshall. Years after their retirements, we look back on their careers with a grin.*

## MARK FIDRYCH

In 1976, Mark Fidrych wasn't just a pitcher. He was baseball's must-see event. Long, lanky and gawky, Fidrych earned the nickname "The Bird" because of his resemblance to the *Sesame Street* character Big Bird. His statistics alone were memorable — a 19-9 record with a league-leading 2.34 ERA. But to define him by stats alone would be just as myopic as remembering NBA showman Dennis Rodman solely for his rebounds. His pitching style was distinct; his impromptu hands-on groundskeeping and his dialogue with the baseball captured the country's attention. Hunched over with his cap low and shaggy hair framing his face, he instructed the baseball where to go. This was after he had already dropped to one knee and filled the hole in front of the pitching rubber before each inning.

"People thought I was strange," Fidrych said. "I didn't think anything of it until they started saying, 'You know what you are doing out there?' I would say, 'Yeah, I am pitching. I am filling up the hole. You want me to get the grounds crew out here and stop the game every time?'"

As for those psychiatry sessions with the baseball?

"I know they thought I was weird, talking to the ball. But I was talking to myself out there, getting some nerves out," Fidrych said.

Fidrych refused to throw a ball that had given up a hit and threw back balls that had "dents." Fans went crazy for his persona. Girls would follow him to the barbershop and scoop up his freshly shorn locks as souvenirs.

Sabotaged by a torn rotator cuff, Fidrych won just 10 more games after his magical '76 season. He died in an accident at age 54 at his Massachusetts farm in 2009, but his toothy smile, fanatical following and strange gait made him impossible to forget.

"In the two years he was here," legend Al Kaline said, "he was probably the most popular Detroit Tiger there has ever been."

> **"When you're a winner you're always happy, but if you're happy as a loser you'll always be a loser."**
> —Fidrych

## LUIS TIANT

Before there was Orlando "El Duque" Hernandez, there was Luis Tiant. He left Cuba in 1961, made his Major League debut in 1964, and over the next 19 years became one of baseball's best pitchers, winning 229 games.

Tiant used a pitching motion that seemed to mock batters when he turned his back to them mid-delivery.

"I didn't do it for show. I did it to get batters out," Tiant said. "Players would tell me, 'We can't tell where the ball is coming from.'"

Most teammates don't remember "El Tiante" just for his success or delivery — they remember him for the cigars. He smoked stogies in the shower, a habit that began as a 18-year-old in the Mexican League. During his career, which began in Cleveland — where he threw four straight shutouts in 1968 — and peaked in the 1970s with the Red Sox, teammates would try to put out his $1 cigars by splashing water on them, but nobody seems to recall anyone ever succeeding. After retiring in 1982, Tiant introduced his own signature line of "23 Series" cigars.

While his smoking habits were maddening to some, his pitching delivery was unfathomable to most. After altering his delivery prior to the '68 season, Tiant was nothing short of a contortionist. He would turn his back to hitters while hesitating with a pregnant pause before firing a pitch. It was like he morphed into a human hiccup. The fact that he had more pitches — fastball, curveball, slider, knuckleball — than a used-car salesman didn't hurt either.

"Oh, I was looking. I might look at the last minute, yes, but I have an idea where I want to throw the ball," Tiant said. "Home plate is where it has always been. All of your life you throw the ball across home plate, so I know where it is."

## DIZZY DEAN

According to the *Merriam-Webster Dictionary*, "dizzy" is defined as "causing giddiness or mental confusion" or "extremely fast," and both meanings fit Dizzy Dean. The St. Louis Cardinals' hurler made a lot of people happy, angry and confused. The Hall of Famer won 150 games during his 12-year career, including 30 for the '34 Cards. When an arm injury forced him to retire, he said that there would never be another player like him — and he was correct. He was at his best in the 1930s, and specifically in 1934 when he and his brother, Paul, teamed up to win 49 games for the "Gashouse Gang."

As a pinch-runner in the World Series against the Tigers that same season, Dean was beaned while trying to break up a double play. He was placed on a stretcher, babbling as he went to a local hospital. Dizzy took pride in the next day's headline, which read: "X-ray of Dean's Head Reveals Nothing."

After retiring, Dean enjoyed one of the best broadcasting runs ever by an ex-player, filling the airwaves from 1941–65. In the booth, he had NFL playboy Joe Namath's bravado and wacky broadcaster Harry Caray's syntax. His country grammar endeared him to fans, inventing phrases like "Slud into the base" and "argyin with an umpire."

Upon Dean's death in 1974, columnist Jim Murray wrote, "If I know Diz, he'll be calling God 'podner' someplace today. I hope there's golf courses or a card game or a slugger who's a sucker for a low outside fastball for Diz. He might have been what baseball's all about."

## CURTIS LESKANIC

A native of Pittsburgh, Curtis Leskanic became a hard-throwing, right-handed pitcher with a daffy smile and a rare, child-like enthusiasm for the game. He bounced around the Major Leagues early in his career — making notable stops with the Rockies, Brewers and Red Sox — before his quirkiness drew national attention. Leskanic admitted that he shaved his right arm to reduce wind resistance, believing that it added 3 miles per hour to his fastball. Sometimes, when trying to ensure that he was a cut above the competition, he shaved his legs as well.

"It makes me feel free and more aerody-namic," Leskanic said.

No wonder former teammates called him "Psycho" early in his career.

Leskanic's grooming habits weren't the only source of attention. He used props as well. He always kept a Pittsburgh Steelers helmet in his locker and once, after a par-ticularly bad road trip, he put it on and ran naked on the treadmill in the club-house to lighten the mood.

"He didn't stop until everyone on the team saw him," said former Colorado Rockies teammate Jerry Dipoto. "Guys couldn't stop laughing."

With the Brewers, Leskanic brought an electronic hunting device to Spring Training that made the sounds of a yelping coyote. "That's just my arm barking," he quipped.

Leskanic, who had a career 4.36 ERA and 50 wins, rode off into the sunset with the Boston Red Sox, winning a World Series ring in 2004. In a vintage Leskanic moment in the clincher over the St. Louis Cardinals, he made mock snow angels in the outfield as his teammates celebrated the franchise's first title since 1918.

> "The problem with being Comeback Player of the Year is it means you have to go somewhere before you can come back."
> —Blyleven

## BERT BLYLEVEN

Appropriate for a man who buckled teammates' knees with laughter and threw fans for a loop with his entertaining style in the broadcast booth, Bert Blyleven's best pitch was a curveball. Blyleven began his Big League career in 1970, winning 10 games for the Minnesota Twins as a 20-year-old. He finished with 287 wins and two World Series rings.

"He's one of the toughest guys I faced in my career," said Royals Hall of Fame third baseman George Brett.

Blyleven was a different sort — funny, temperamental and candid. If he thought it, he said it. Or did it. Blyleven's irreverent opinions brought attention and trouble. The Twins tired of the right-hander once, shipping him off to the Texas Rangers in 1976. He threw a no-hitter for Texas and also infamously flashed his middle finger, getting shipped to the Pittsburgh Pirates in 1977 and eventually back to the Twins by way of Cleveland. He was always in the middle of controversy, and prank wars, including the famous "hot foot," in which he would light an unsuspecting team-mate's shoe on fire.

By 1986, Blyleven lamented the vanishing role of the clubhouse cut-up. Of course, he did it on the same day that he mooned the cameraman in the first take of a Minnesota Twins' team picture, stealing a page out of brash NFL quarterback Jim McMahon's playbook.

"One reason there are fewer [cut-ups] is because of you guys, the media. Players hold back because every move they make is written about," Blyleven said. "Another is free agency. Now guys just don't stay together as long as they used to."

Blyleven made a successful transition into the Twins' broadcast booth after his playing career ended in 1992. In that role, he gained fame for, among other things, eating worms during a Parkinson's charity event and his frequent use of telestrator circles. He gave fans a few seconds of goofy attention, which prompted many to carry "Circle Me Bert" signs to the ballpark.

## ROGER McDOWELL

When *Seinfeld* writers went searching for a laugh from the sports world in 1992, they hit a home run with a send-up of the Oliver Stone film *JFK*. New York Mets pitcher and comic-relief specialist Roger McDowell — named to the Mets' 40th Anniversary All-Amazin' Team as a right-handed reliever in 2002 — played a critical part in the script. It went down like this: Characters Newman and Kramer ridiculed Mets first baseman Keith Hernandez as he left Shea Stadium following a critical error. Kramer suddenly felt spit on his neck before it allegedly ricocheted into Newman. In a terrific spoof of the Abraham Zapruder film, Jerry Seinfeld determines that it's scientifically impossible for both men to have been hit by the same spit. There was, he concluded, a second spitter — Roger McDowell — who was exacting revenge against Kramer for pouring beer on his head during the game.

"It wasn't much of a part: it was a non-speaking part. But I did throw the 'magic loogie,'" McDowell said.

McDowell's humor usually leaned less toward conspiracy and more in the direction of tomfoolery. He was the king of the "hot foot" prank. And how many times have you seen players hanging out over the dugout rail with bubble gum bubbles on their caps? That was a McDowell classic. Once, to lighten the mood during a nationally televised game, he wore his entire uniform upside down — pants for a shirt, shirt for pants, shoes on hands.

A classic McDowell gag came in 1994. Cincinnati Reds Owner Marge Schott made an off-color comment about players who wear earrings, implying that they weren't manly. McDowell, then pitching for the Los Angeles Dodgers, bought earrings for his entire team entering a series against the Reds.

## DAN QUISENBERRY

Baseball is a sport defined by angles and oddities. Dan Quisenberry combined both brilliantly. A true sidearmer, the arm slot of his delivery was perpendicular to his body.

"I found a delivery in my flaw," Quisenberry said of his near-underhand style that more closely resembled a fast-pitch softball toss than a Big League star.

Although his fastball rarely topped 83 miles per hour, he turned bats into sawdust, inducing a battery of groundballs. Hitters were always convinced that they could rake against him, and Quisenberry played on their egos, earning 244 saves over his 12-year career while finishing in the top five in Cy Young voting five times.

"I want to thank all the pitchers who couldn't go nine innings, and Royals Manager Dick Howser, who wouldn't let them," said Quisenberry after winning the 1982 Rolaids Award as the American League's top reliever.

How many other relief pitchers can you name who have won two league championships and published just as many poetry books? Quisenberry would often work his extensive knowledge into his interviews. After blowing one particular save opportunity, Quisenberry was asked if there could be any worse way to lose a ballgame. He managed to reel off 20 things, including a natural disaster. After the Philadelphia Phillies tagged Quisenberry in the 1980 World Series, he quipped, "We have our backs against the Berlin Wall — east side."

Teammate Mark Gubicza marveled at how Quisenberry could tell a joke — elaborate and ridiculous as it might be — while keeping a straight face.

Tragically, Quisenberry died of brain cancer in 1998. A few days before his death, he held a press conference at Kaufmann Stadium to talk about the disease. The man who had saved so many games couldn't save his own life, but he inspired many others with his success, kindness and sense of humor.

# "Natural grass is a wonderful thing for little bugs and sinkerball pitchers." —Quisenberry

## BILLY LOES

Introductions, please: Billy Loes, meet Logic. Logic, Billy Loes. The two were strangers throughout Loes's colorful Major League career, which spanned from 1950–61. The right-hander was a successful pitcher for the Brooklyn Dodgers, but his quips have long overshadowed his stats. His most famous came during the 1952 World Series, when Loes muffed a groundball that was hit back to him.

"Lost it in the sun," Loes explained.

That quote has endured for six decades, popping up as a one-liner everywhere from slow-pitch softball games to Little League contests. And there were others, as well. Before the start of the '52 World Series, Loes informed the press that the rival Yankees would win in seven games, which was the ultimate result. When confronted by his manager, he said he was, indeed, misquoted — he had predicted the Yankees to win in six.

Aside from being an ace prognosticator, Loes was also a pretty good pitcher. He went 50-26 in his six seasons in Brooklyn. When he landed with the Orioles in 1956 as a classic reclamation project after flaming out in Brooklyn, he won 12 games the following year.

"Never win 20 games because they will expect you to do it every year," Loes said.

Paul Richards, his manager in Baltimore, was ridiculed for gambling on a retread, especially one who was essentially uncoachable. "What have I got to lose?" Richards said.

Certainly not his sense of humor.

## DR. MIKE MARSHALL

Magnificent. Contentious. Both are apt descriptions of Mike Marshall's Big League career. In 1974, he won the National League Cy Young Award, appearing in 106 games out of the Dodgers' bullpen and finishing 83 contests. He worked 208.1 innings.

Although Marshall's durability engendered respect among his peers, he couldn't drum up more than indifference from most fans. Marshall was not like any other player of his time. For starters, he was a converted shortstop. Signed by the Philadelphia Phillies in 1960, he couldn't deal with the daily back pain caused by a childhood car accident. He requested to become a pitcher, and the club asked him to leave. Marshall persevered and reached the Majors with the Tigers in 1967. By 1971, he led the NL in games finished and was studying the arm and the human body.

He was the only active Big League hurler with a doctorate, having earned a Ph.D from Michigan State in Exercise Physiology in 1978. His studies led him to question everything that was taught to pitchers regarding proper mechanics.

"I had decided not to listen to anybody," Marshall explained. "I didn't have everything figured out yet, but I knew what they were telling me was contrary to everything I learned about physics. From then on there was only one pitching coach I'd listen to: Isaac Newton."

Marshall was best when left alone. Manager Gene Mauch identified with the deep thinker as the right-hander blossomed in Montreal, foreshadowing his tireless 1974 season with the Dodgers. But Marshall's intellect created enemies. Pitchers didn't like that he didn't attend meetings, and owners detested his strong union involvement. As a result, his career ended prematurely. Still, his 1974 season remains a gem that defied all odds, if not physics.

Paige (second from right)

## SATCHEL PAIGE

Most American icons have had their lives examined so thoroughly that every last biographical detail becomes common knowledge. This makes the air of mystery still hovering about Satchel Paige all the more impressive. According to Larry Tye's book *Satchel*, the pitcher was born Leroy Robert Page in 1906. He most likely earned the nickname "Satchel" as a young boy while working as a porter at the Mobile, Ala., railroad depot, where he made a contraption with a pole that allowed him to carry four bags, or satchels, at once. Others insist it's because he once stole a satchel from the depot, while still others claimed to have called him Satchelfoot for his big feet.

Whatever the origin of his unique sobriquet, Paige became a legend in the Negro Leagues. For 21 years he starred for various clubs — most notably the Pittsburgh Crawfords and Kansas City Monarchs. Paige would pitch three times a week, drawing huge crowds that were mesmerized by his work. That explains why he got a cut of the gate.

During barnstorming tours in the 1930s and '40s, he gained the respect and admiration of Big Leaguers. Dizzy Dean called him the greatest pitcher who ever lived, and the Yankees decided Joe DiMaggio was ready for a promotion when he got a hit off Paige.

Yet for all his skill, Paige's dynamic personality is what endures. He was a blend of Yoda and Yogi, making perfect sense with imperfect sentences. When he finally reached the Big Leagues with the Indians in 1948, Paige was praised by writers after a shutout victory and told he might win the Rookie of the Year Award.

"Well, 22 years is a long time to be a rookie," said Paige.

On Sept. 25, 1965, Paige threw his last pitch in the Bigs at the age of 59 for the Kansas City Athletics.

## CHAPTER 2

# LEFT-HANDED COMPLEMENT

*When baseball diamonds were first being laid out across the country the habit was to have the batters face east so that the setting sun was not in their eyes. When most pitchers stood from the stretch on the mound, their throwing arms were on the north side of the hill — except for those rare left-handers. These "southpaws" attacked hitters from a whole different angle. Only about 10 percent of the population is left-handed, yet in the search for colorful baseball personalities, southpaws provide a neon light. Bill "Spaceman" Lee contributed out-of-this-world quotes and comments while Al Hrabosky stomped around, staging a Broadway theatre show before pitching. Lefty Gomez threw out one-liners as great as his pitches, and Fernando Valenzuela inflicted a pandemic on an entire West Coast population.*

## BILL LEE

When it comes to free spirits, Bill Lee is in his own galaxy. Lee was a decent pitcher, winning 119 games in his 14-year career, including a decade-long run that left him beloved in Boston. Still, he's remembered not as a pitcher, but as a symbol for the counterculture of the late 1960s and early '70s. He earned the nickname "Spaceman" from Red Sox teammate John Kennedy because he was considered a flake.

In truth, Lee was just a free-thinking original.

The socially conscious Lee attracted liberal, college-age fans with his rebellious side. One of Lee's most famous run-ins with the baseball establishment came when he admitted to using marijuana, a hot-button issue at the center of the generation gap. Commissioner Bowie Kuhn fined him $250 after Lee admitted that he sprinkled the drug on his buckwheat pancakes. He loved songwriter Warren Zevon, who eventually wrote a song titled "Bill Lee." He spoke out on political issues, including school busing in Boston. His willingness to question authority put him at odds with Red Sox Manager Don Zimmer, whom Lee referred to as "a gerbil." Zimmer disliked Lee so much that he influenced a trade that sent Lee to the Expos, where he helped lead his new club to the 1981 playoffs.

Lee was fascinating because, unlike some eccentrics, when he crossed the white lines he might as well have been carrying a briefcase. Although a lefty by birth and in politics, Lee was a traditionalist on the mound. He despised the designated hitter and AstroTurf. In the end, Lee's career met its demise when he walked out in protest from the Montreal Expos following the release of teammate Rodney Scott.

"Baseball is the belly button of America," Lee wrote in his autobiography *Wrong Stuff* in 1984. "If you straighten out the belly button, the rest of the country will follow suit."

## FRITZ PETERSON

Most memorable trades in baseball history involve players being swapped for other players rather than players swapping *with* players. Yet in 1973, Fritz Peterson traded wives and lives with Yankees teammate Mike Kekich, dogs and kids included. The experiment failed horribly for Kekich, whose wife, Susanne, eventually married Peterson. The bizarre arrangement, which severely strained the players' relationship, was revealed during Spring Training.

"We may have to call off Family Day," Yankees GM Lee MacPhail conceded.

The subsequent negative press didn't help Peterson. A solid pitcher who averaged 16 wins per year from 1968–72, he was booed soundly on the road, and his play dipped. He won just eight games in 1973.

The idea of Peterson as a villain was incongruous. He was, by all accounts, a clubhouse favorite. Teammate Sparky Lyle called him "The Master" at pranks. One time, Peterson set Lyle up in elaborate fashion. He told Lyle he would give him a ride, pointing out his rental car in the parking lot. As Lyle tried to get into the car, Peterson paged the real owner, who thought his vehicle was being stolen. Peterson also pulled off a doozy on Moose Skowron. On fake letterhead from the Baseball Hall of Fame, he asked Skowron to donate his pacemaker after his death.

Peterson is the rare Yankee who never reached the postseason with the Bombers. He called his Yankees teams, "mediocre at best, pathetic at worst." One of his most noteworthy games: He was the starter for Cleveland on "10 Cent Beer Night," when the debauchery caused a forfeit.

Detailing his life in his book *Mickey Mantle is Going To Heaven*, Peterson criticized Joe DiMaggio and accused Whitey Ford of doctoring the ball. The book, like Peterson, is an interesting contradiction.

Peterson with ex-wife and children

## AL HRABOSKY

Before even throwing a pitch, Al Hrabosky put on a show. Nicknamed the "Mad Hungarian," Hrabosky would stomp off the mound toward second before starting an inning, eyes wild as sin. He would pound the ball into his glove, then turn back toward home plate looking as if he had been inhabited by a demon.

"It happened out of desperation," said Hrabosky, who saved 97 games and had a 3.10 ERA in 13 seasons. "I figured if it didn't work, it might accelerate my exit, but I had nothing to lose."

Teammates and fans fed off the charge. Opponents? Nope. Bill Madlock once walked out of the batter's box, prompting Hrabosky to start his routine over. Hrabosky eventually fired at the vacant box, inciting a brawl. Hrabosky symbolized the wild 1970s. He grew his hair long and had a Fu Manchu mustache. He even wore a silver ring, calling it "The Gypsy Rose of Death."

Hrabosky evolved into this character, feeling he needed an edge to get hitters out. He looked wild when he pitched, thus the root of the nickname given to him by a team publicist. And even this was doctored since Hrabosky was not a native Hungarian.

In 1977, when Cards Manager Vern Rapp made Hrabosky shave, the pitcher wondered aloud how he could intimidate when he "looked like a golf pro." Hrabosky turned his unique personality into a TV career with the Cardinals, but no, he doesn't slap his microphone and widen his eyes before each broadcast.

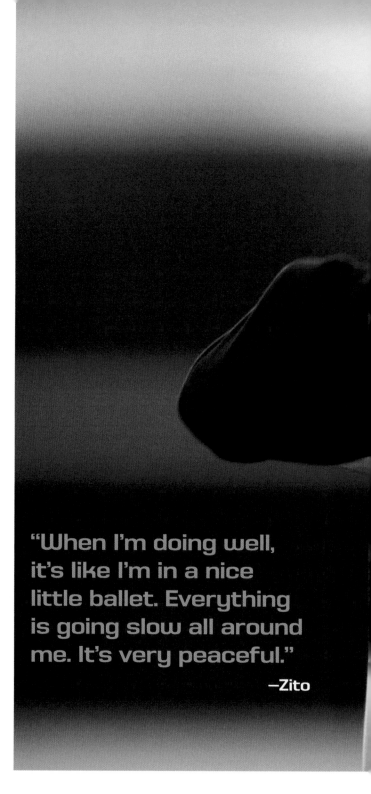

"When I'm doing well, it's like I'm in a nice little ballet. Everything is going slow all around me. It's very peaceful."

—Zito

## BARRY ZITO

Well before Barry Zito became the highest-paid pitcher in Big League history in 2007, he was among the most eccentric. The southpaw was laidback, open-minded, funny and yet deathly serious on the hill. Picture this: a Big Leaguer traveling with his lucky stuffed animals, love beads and satin pillows. That was Zito early in his career with the Oakland A's. Yet for all his zaniness, there was nothing weird about his capturing a Cy Young Award, while winning 23 games on the strength of a big-bending curveball.

"He was strange, no question about it," former teammate Jason Giambi said. "But he wasn't a flake."

Zito likes solving problems with creative solutions, but that has caused some bumps along his journey. In his first year across the bay with the San Francisco Giants, just months after signing a record $126-million, seven-year contract, he showed up to Spring Training with a radical new pitching motion. To some, it was just part of Zito's creativity. But nobody paying the checks

for the Giants thought it was funny. He quickly changed back to his original delivery.

Zito explained it thusly: "It's like the *Bull Durham* quote, when he has mildew on his shower shoes, and Kevin Costner says: 'If you win 20 in The Show, that's colorful. But until then, you're a slob.'"

Through slumps, Zito learned he's better when he doesn't try to be anyone but himself. And if that means his hair wouldn't know what to make of a comb without a name tag, so be it.

# FERNANDO VALENZUELA

The 1981 Major League season was shortened by a players' strike, but an unknown Mexican pitcher made sure the campaign wasn't remembered for that. Fernando Valenzuela created a national craze. He was the bull, nicknamed "El Toro" by fans for his pudgy build.

He spawned "Fernandomania" with his rags-to-riches story and immediate success. Valenzuela was discovered by scout Mike Brito, who found him by accident while scouting another Mexican player. Soon, the left-hander from Etchohuaquila had Los Angeles in a frenzy. He won his first 10 decisions in the Bigs, en route to 173 career victories.

"It would be difficult to win every game I pitch," he said, before hinting at his ego. "But not impossible."

Valenzuela's screwball, and the manner in which he delivered it, made him unique. He would kick his leg up high, turn his head to the heavens, then close his eyes before delivering hell to hitters. It was part Luis Tiant, part magic trick. That it was coming from the left side only made the delivery more unusual. His control wasn't bad, but he didn't have to throw a lot of strikes with his trademark screwball. Fellow pitcher Bobby Castillo taught him the pitch, which requires the unusual action of turning the wrist away from the body, begging for an injury.

Valenzuela pitched well into his 40s, continuing his career in the Mexican Pacific League following his retirement from the Bigs. That he performed with such childlike enthusiasm — he once served as the Dodgers' batboy — made his story even easier to love.

"That's what's so beautiful about Fernando," Dodgers pitching coach Ron Perranoski said during the magical 1981 season that saw Valenzuela win both the Rookie of the Year and Cy Young awards. "Things like him just don't happen."

"I talked to the ball a lot of times in my career. I yelled, 'Go foul. Go foul.'"

**—Gomez**

## LEFTY GOMEZ

Vernon "Lefty" Gomez said he always preferred to be lucky rather than good. Nicknamed "El Goofy," Gomez is considered the original flake by writers who covered him.

Gomez was a wildly successful pitcher with the New York Yankees, winning 26 games one season and leading the league in ERA twice and in strikeouts three times. He also went 6-0 in World Series games, part of a Hall of Fame career that spanned from 1930–43. But he is better known for his self-deprecating quips. One of his better lines came at a speaking engagement after the United States landed its first astronauts on the moon in 1969. He explained that the astronauts were confused by an unidentified white object flying around.

"I knew immediately what it was. That was the home run ball hit off me by Jimmie Foxx in 1937," he deadpanned. He said of Foxx, "He had muscles in his hair."

Gomez once shook off catcher Bill Dickey so much with Foxx batting that the backstop wondered if he needed more fingers before finally asking Gomez what he wanted to throw.

"I don't wanna throw him nothin'," Gomez explained. "Maybe he'll just get tired of waitin' and leave."

That was Gomez at his comedic best. When asked how hard he threw on the radar gun, he said his fastball rarely hit the mitt because it was constantly getting hit. A notoriously bad hitter, he made fun of himself plenty for that, too, once saying years after retirement, "I never broke a bat until last year when I was backing out of the garage." Gomez won 189 games during his 14-year career, but his most impressive feat might have been bringing out Joe DiMaggio's wit and making a joke at his friend Lou Gehrig's expense.

"Hell, Lou," Gomez said, "it took 15 years to get you out of a game. Sometimes I'm out in 15 minutes."

## CHAPTER 3

# LEADERS OF MEN

*Big League managers aren't just leaders — they are amateur psychologists and life coaches. They are dartboards for agitated fans and, in some cases, for their players. To pull the strings in a dugout, a skipper needs to know the game. But there are different ways to get results. Tommy Lasorda brought everything but pom-poms into the clubhouse during his run with the Dodgers, motivating players with corny tales and a pumped fist. Others, like Earl Weaver and Billy Martin, steered with an equal blend of venom and gruff. Some, such as John McGraw, took a more nuanced approach. And then there were those who fixed broken seasons with fractured syntax — like the incomparable Casey Stengel.*

Stengel
(right)

## CASEY STENGEL

Groomed to work in the Major Leagues, Casey Stengel was a baseball genius, fighting for his team, fighting with fans and fighting for championships before finishing his career as an amusing jester with the bumbling Mets. Stengel won seven World Series with the Yankees, deftly managing a museum-worthy collection of talent. His fingerprints were all over the team's aggressive running game — nobody went from first to third better than Casey during his playing career — and he maximized his roster with his novel platooning of players. But he could also be mean and grumpy.

"I always wondered why he was so nice to me, and I think it was because he thought [mistakenly] I was related to former Yankees coach Buck Herzog," said Hall of Fame Manager Whitey Herzog.

During his time in the Bronx, Stengel was closest to Yogi Berra, Billy Martin and Mickey Mantle, loving them like sons. He understood locker-room politics, and also figured out the media, making time for reporters and providing memorable quotes and photo ops (it didn't hurt that his weathered face looked like a winking catcher's mitt). Stengel's lasting legacy was being unintentionally funny in his long sessions with the press. He once quipped, "I want to thank all my players for giving me the honor of being what I was."

After years of competing for World Series crowns, Stengel ended his illustrious managerial career as the face of the 1962 Mets, the worst team in history. The not-so-Amazin's were historically awful and colorful — "a disaster," Stengel said — endearing themselves to New York City as lovable losers during their debut season in the National League. And no one was more lovable on that squad than Stengel, who garnered goodwill even while poking fun at the ineptitude of his own players.

"Can't anybody here play this game?" Stengel famously wondered during that tumultuous campaign.

## BOBBY VALENTINE

Few baseball men have ever been as sure of their intellect as Bobby Valentine. His faith in his ability annoyed some at times, but his brains and individualism made him successful on two continents. With the Rangers in 1986, he used a satellite dish to watch other teams instead of trusting an advance scout, winning 87 games. Later, he led the Mets to the 2000 World Series. In Japan, he revitalized a franchise and inspired such loyalty with the Chiba Lotte fans that they campaigned to keep him. Meanwhile, it took the Mets a few dismal years to get back on track after Valentine left in 2002.

Skills aside, he's often remembered for sporting a fake mustache in a clandestine effort to help his team. On June 9, 1999, Valentine's Mets were playing Toronto. He had recently lost three coaches from his staff against his wishes. In the 12th inning, Valentine was ejected after arguing a call. Watching from the clubhouse, Robin Ventura urged Valentine to return to the dugout, saying the new coaches had no idea who was even in the bullpen.

Valentine wore sunglasses and a ratty cap, and put eye black stickers above his lip. When Edgardo Alfonzo hit a pop-up, the cameras spied Valentine with his arms folded across his chest. While his players laughed — levity that perhaps helped produce a win — MLB didn't find it funny. Valentine was fined $10,000 and suspended three games. "People give me more credit than I deserve in some things I did and a lot less credit than I deserve in other things that I did," Valentine said. "That's just the way life is."

## EARL WEAVER

Before there was VORP and WHIP, there was Earl Weaver — the numbers-crunching manager who steered by stats that hadn't yet been popularized. Weaver was ornery and competitive, admitting that he was the sorest loser who ever lived.

"I take everything personal," Weaver said.

He left behind a wake of impressions during his 17-plus seasons managing the Orioles. Staunch in his principles, Weaver kept his distance from players, bragging about how he spoke fewer than 30 words to superstars Brooks Robinson and Frank Robinson (no relation) during their time together. He trusted his starting pitchers and played for the three-run homer. He was called "Dr. Longball," among other unprintable nicknames.

Weaver was respected, but never universally embraced in Baltimore. In one team meeting, Weaver urged his men to trust each other offensively. He said he never recalled making the last out. Ace Jim Palmer — a Hall of Famer with Hollywood looks whose "complexes had complexes," according to writer Thomas Boswell — said, "That's because they always pinch-hit for you."

Weaver's passionate arguments with umpires were must-see TV, featuring kicked dirt, sideways caps and enough expletives to make comedian George Carlin blush. He holds the American League record for ejections with 98, including two in a doubleheader.

"Is this as good as you're gonna get?" he yelled at one umpire. "I just want to know if this is the best we can expect."

# LEADERS OF MEN

## SPARKY ANDERSON

During the tumultuous 1970s and '80s, George "Sparky" Anderson was a staunch conservative who had no interest in long hair. He didn't understand those around him who didn't respect authority. Yet Anderson did not rule with an iron fist. Play-Doh was more like it. With Cincinnati's Big Red Machine of 1975–76 — the last National League team to win back-to-back titles — Sparky coddled the stars. He openly set different rules for players like Pete Rose, Johnny Bench, Joe Morgan and Tony Perez. His strategy was simple, and unthinkable to many of his egomaniacal predecessors throughout history.

"There's two kinds of managers," Anderson said during his Hall of Fame induction speech. "One that ain't very smart. He gets bad players, loses games and gets fired. Then there was somebody like me that was a genius. I got good players, stayed out of the way, let 'em win a lot."

Anderson certainly had his share of distinct foibles. He earned the nickname "Captain Hook" for removing starting pitchers at the very first sign of weakness, bead of sweat or chipped fingernail. He gave his ballplayers a wide breadth in the clubhouse, and they responded. His self-deprecating personality didn't hurt, either. After he was let go by the Reds, he appeared on the sitcom *WKRP in Cincinnati*, getting fired again.

He landed in Detroit, where he revived the franchise. He was no stranger to hyperbole, talking about Kirk Gibson as the next Mickey Mantle. And he is remembered for becoming the first manager to win a World Series in both the NL and AL, guiding the Tigers to the 1984 crown.

"There was one man responsible for putting this together," said former Tigers shortstop Alan Trammell during a reunion in 2009. "Sparky, we love ya!"

Anderson (center)

## JOHN McGRAW

Some choose Connie Mack. Others say Casey Stengel. But when it comes to the debate of the greatest manager ever, John McGraw is always, at the very least, in the conversation. He was a star player before becoming a tenacious manager, a loyal friend, a hated enemy and a pioneer. At the turn of the century, when the country embraced baseball as the national pastime, McGraw was the right man in the right place at the right time. He took over the New York Giants, a spiraling franchise with bad players, and turned them into a machine of excellence, intelligence and athleticism, winning three World Series.

As Charles C. Alexander wrote in *John McGraw*, "He epitomized what a baseball manager was supposed to be: smart, pugnacious, tough and demanding with his players." Thus, the nickname "Little Napoleon." He taught the game, and was never bashful about taking credit for everything that went well.

As a player, he insisted that he, along with teammate Wee Willie Keeler, invented the hit-and-run strategy. "The Baltimore Chop?" McGraw was part of its creation, too, working with other players to have the Baltimore groundskeeper make the dirt in front of home plate as hard as a rock to create extra hits. He showed how a game could also be a business. But he was a paradox, oddly mixing generous pats on the backside with knives in the back.

Beyond showing confidence in himself and his team — especially in pitcher Christy Mathewson — McGraw picked fights with umpires, fans and entire cities. Under McGraw, the Giants became the team that everyone loved to hate, and the club's games became can't-miss affairs. His players joked that McGraw started more fights, and finished fewer, than anyone. McGraw summed it up best when he said, "I think we can win if my brains hold out."

**"One percent of ballplayers are leaders of men. The other 99 percent are followers of women." —McGraw**

## TOMMY LASORDA

It was October 2009 at Dodger Stadium and the "Boys in Blue" were pushing for a playoff spot, yet the loudest cheer of the night came when former skipper Tommy Lasorda appeared on the JumboTron. To many, Lasorda — who led the team to world titles in 1981 and '88 — will always be the face of the Los Angeles Dodgers.

"I bleed Dodger blue," Lasorda said. "And when I die, I am going to the big Dodger in the sky."

Part father figure, part cheerleader, Lasorda still drives Dodgers fans wild.

"Tommy Lasorda changed managing," former player Bobby Valentine said. "The 'do as you're told — yes sir' mentality began to change with him [in 1976]."

Lasorda's motivational speeches were legendary. He was never afraid to celebrate with his men or offer a hug. He defended his players and himself if challenged by an opponent. He once fought the Phillie Phanatic, and his rants against foes like the Padres' Kurt Bevacqua and the Cubs' Dave Kingman will be YouTube classics for years. He also had a biting sense of humor, once joking that Rick Monday and Manny Mota were so old, they were waiters at the Last Supper.

Lasorda loved every minute of it. "How can you get burned out doing something you love?" Lasorda said. "I ask you, have you ever gotten tired of kissing a pretty girl?"

"When we win, I'm so happy, I eat a lot. When we lose, I'm so depressed, I eat a lot. When we're rained out, I'm so disappointed, I eat a lot." —Lasorda

## BILLY MARTIN

As a player, Billy Martin was a favorite of Yankees Manager Casey Stengel. His contributions could be hard to quantify, but when he played, the team tended to win. The spindly second baseman was the classic grinder — an overachiever and an agitator. He went through life with a huge chip on his shoulder. His feelings of insecurity created a tidal wave of classic confrontations and endless job changes, namely from battles with Yankees Owner George Steinbrenner.

The flying fists and paranoia overshadow his tactical brilliance as a manager. Martin spent countless hours preparing imaginary strategies that could be used against rival teams, work that he ultimately employed to win games.

When he arrived in New York as a ballplayer in 1950, he predicted that he would one day lead a Big League team. Twenty-seven years later, he guided the Yankees to a title amid such chaos that it inspired one of the classic baseball books, *Ladies and Gentlemen, The Bronx is Burning*.

Martin managed five different franchises, winning division titles with Minnesota, Detroit, New York and Oakland. He was a master tactician who motivated his players through intimidation. And occasionally, the threat of violence was real. He traded punches with players in Detroit and Minnesota, lost a brawl with New York pitcher Ed Whitson, and famously tussled with a traveling marshmallow salesman in 1979.

He went after Reggie Jackson in a dugout at Fenway Park and suspended the superstar for bunting when given the sign to swing. He called Steinbrenner a liar, although the two had repaired their relationship by the time Martin died on Christmas Day in 1989.

"He had his ups and downs, but he was a Yankee, heart and soul," former shortstop Bucky Dent said. "He was a winner, and nobody can fault him for that."

## DON ZIMMER

Don Zimmer won 885 games as a Big League manager. He took the Cubs to the playoffs in 1989 when they were picked to finish last. He changed the Padres' culture by relaxing the dress code and allowing beer on team flights. But he will forever be linked to a pair of Red Sox pitchers: Pedro Martinez and Bill "Spaceman" Lee. When Zimmer was his manager, Lee called him a "gerbil," which would be an incredible insult if it weren't so spot on. And all Martinez did was push the then-72-year-old to the ground during a playoff melee in 2003.

The day of the 2003 clash at Fenway, Martinez was pitching for Boston, while Zimmer was the bench coach for the Yankees. Martinez threw a ball behind Karim Garcia. After a hard slide from Garcia and a Roger Clemens inside fastball to Boston's Manny Ramirez, Zimmer lunged toward Pedro as the benches cleared. Martinez grabbed him and pushed him to the ground. The hurler blamed the incident on Zimmer as recently as 2009, saying, "He was trying to punch my mouth and told me a couple of bad words about my mom." Zimmer's fury could be traced to his own 1953 beaning. He had a steel plate placed in his head after getting hit — the root, he believes, of his goofiness. And a couple of years before the Pedro incident, New York's Chuck Knoblauch fouled a ball off of Zimmer's head, prompting Zimmer to wear a Yankees army helmet the next day.

Zimmer's profile grew as New York Manager Joe Torre's sidekick, and he helped tutor Joe Girardi, who took the managerial reins in 2008. He became part comic relief, part sage, an endless source of quips.

"If Joe [Torre] orders a hit-and-run and it works, I pat him on the back and say, 'Smart move,'" Zimmer once said. "If it doesn't work, I go down and hang around the water cooler."

## CHAPTER 4

# RAISE THE GOOF

*They don't always respect baseball's conservative traditions or conform to its many rituals, but these idiosyncratic players provide some of the game's most memorable moments, as well as tons of laughs. Dante Bichette's annual March surprise — long hair or short, Strongman or Fat Elvis? — was often the highlight of Rockies Spring Training. Manny Ramirez surprised teammates and fans when he took a bathroom break in the Green Monster — during a game. Pedro Martinez shocked fans when he said he would like to plunk Babe Ruth in the posterior. And Rickey Henderson all but invented the art of talking in third person. The acts could be narcissistic, but they certainly weren't boring.*

## PEDRO MARTINEZ

With nearly as many moods as he had pitches, Pedro Martinez could be alarmingly candid, impressively intellectual and annoyingly diva-like — all during a single press conference. Case in point, he held an epic media session during the 2009 World Series as a member of the Phillies, bearing his soul for nearly 20 minutes on topics ranging from his Major League dreams hatched under a mango tree in the Dominican Republic to being hated in the Bronx. Never particularly modest, Martinez pronounced himself the most influential player ever to set foot in old Yankee Stadium, presumably ranking himself above local heroes Mickey Mantle, Joe DiMaggio and Babe Ruth.

"I can honestly say that. [It's because of] the way you have used and abused me since I've been coming to Yankee Stadium just because I wore a red uniform, just like this [Phillies uniform], while playing for Boston," Martinez said while back in the Bronx during the '09 Fall Classic.

It was as a member of the Red Sox that he said the Yankees were his "daddy" after beating him. That off-the-cuff admission inspired "Who's your daddy?" chants at Yankee Stadium. Although he can be a cold-blooded competitor on the mound, Martinez is well known for his funny side. His smile could light up a clubhouse and his antics kept his teammates loose at every stop in his storied career. With Boston, Martinez traveled with 2-foot-4 Nelson de la Rosa during the 2004 playoffs. He has worn costumes in the dugout, flipped bubble gum into the stands, and performed an impromptu dance routine for fans at Shea Stadium when a sprinkler malfunction delayed one of his starts with the Mets in 2005. Not just another one of the self-proclaimed "Idiots" — those curse-breaking 2004 Red Sox — he was the dominant ace who fueled that memorable club and gave it confidence to embrace its kookiness.

## DANTE BICHETTE

After struggling with consistency with the California Angels and Milwaukee Brewers in the beginning of his career, Dante Bichette joined the expansion Colorado Rockies in 1993 and quickly became a favorite among fans — particularly women — because of his dramatic home runs, long hair and good looks.

When the Rockies nearly lost him as a free agent in 1995, fans held a bake sale outside of Coors Field to raise money to help re-sign the slugger. Bichette was flaky, except when it came to hitting. Before every season, he read Ted Williams' book *The Science of Hitting*. Bichette wasn't much for world events, but he could give a detailed scouting report on the swing of an opponent's backup shortstop. He was loveable because he was always approachable. And he liked the attention. In Spring Training he arrived each year with a new persona, from sleek to Hulk Hogan to a Las Vegas–style Elvis, plump with midnight black hair.

"I don't take myself too seriously," Bichette said.

He also had a misunderstood home run celebration. He would throw his hands back after a longball to mimic his reaction to a winning shot in foosball, but fans felt he was touting his hot bat.

"One of my favorite memories of Dante was when he lumbered after a fly ball and his cap came off. That's when he had the long hair and he couldn't find the ball with his hair covering his eyes," teammate Jerry Dipoto said. "He threw to the wrong base because he couldn't see."

> ## "Never once did I get hit on the head by a fly ball. Once or twice on the shoulder, maybe, but never on the head."
> ### —Herman

## BABE HERMAN

An oddball on a Brooklyn Dodgers team full of them during the 1920s and '30s, Babe Herman played baseball with the enthusiasm of a 6-year-old on Christmas morning. Although Herman could always hit — batting .324 over 13 seasons — it was his bloopers that endeared him to the Flatbush faithful.

Six decades after Herman retired, Jose Canseco took a fly ball off his head. But Herman pulled off similar stunts earlier, deftly letting pop-ups bounce off his noggin and shoulders.

"We didn't have flip glasses in those days and when it got dark enough the sky was murder," Herman said. "When the ball was hit up in the air, there was a black spot you had to pick out of the sun. The black spot was the ball, so you can see sometimes how you could camp under the wrong spot."

For all his misadventures with the glove, his most amazing miscue may have been on the basepaths in 1926, when Herman doubled into a double play. With the bases loaded and backup catcher Mickey O'Neil coaching third base for the first time, Herman bounced a long fly ball off the wall, scoring the game's winning run. As Herman caught up to the closest runner, Chick Fewster, past second base, O'Neil yelled, "Back!" Dazzy Vance, running toward home plate, thought he was talking to him. It produced a classic moment: Vance and Herman sliding into third base from opposite directions as Fewster stood on that very bag.

## TURK WENDELL

Although he made his Big League debut in 1993, Turk Wendell would have fit in nicely with the daffy Brooklyn Dodgers of the 1920s. The right-handed reliever had good stuff and greater antics.

It began at Quinnipiac University in Connecticut, where Wendell wouldn't start an outing until his right fielder tipped his cap back at him. He compiled a 3.93 ERA in 552 career Big League games and had plenty of superstitions. His most famous involved licorice. Wendell would chew pieces of the black candy while he pitched, and between innings he would brush his teeth in the dugout. No runs, no hits, no errors — and no cavities.

Wendell also had a habit of kangaroo hopping over the foul line upon returning to the dugout after each inning. His odd behavior made him a loner at times among his teammates, but not with fans. They adored him because he took time to sign endless autographs. He wasn't afraid to voice unpopular opinions about the game's biggest stars, including Barry Bonds and Sammy Sosa. But Wendell is remembered for more than his biting criticism, although his career certainly had teeth. They were on a necklace around his neck.

"It is my tribute to the animals I have harvested, so that spirit of the animal lives on. I've got a polar bear claw on there that an Eskimo sent me. He said that it was good luck. That is the only thing that I haven't shot. But I've got mountain lion claws, elk teeth, turkey spurs, wild pig teeth and a buffalo tooth."

## MICKEY RIVERS

Some tight-lipped Big Leaguers keep their heads down and deliver one-liners once a decade. Others are genial guys who manage to make us laugh once or twice per season. Then there are guys like Mickey Rivers, a player who fans wanted to pal around with and whom reporters adored for being a wellspring of quotes and controversy. Everything that came out of the longtime center fielder's mouth came out of left field during a 15-year career with the Angels, Yankees and Rangers that spanned the 1970s and '80s, leading his sayings to be categorized as "Riversisms."

Rivers rivaled Yankees legend Yogi Berra for challenging sensibilities — and copy editors. He once said that the key to a good season was staying injury-prone. To maximize his defense, he would stick his finger in the air to check the "windshield factor." Talking about his tough upbringing, he reasoned, "I came from the school of hard knots." Of an opponent that he considered physically unattractive, he blurted, "He's so ugly, when you walk past him your clothes wrinkle." When teammate Reggie Jackson bragged about having a 160 IQ, Rivers retorted, "Out of what, a thousand?"

One of his most famous quotes got tugged and pulled in so many directions that the Texas Rangers reprinted it in the media guide for accuracy's sake. It read: "Ain't no sense worrying about things you got control over, 'cause if you got control over them ain't no sense in worrying. And ain't no sense in worrying about things you got no control over, 'cause if you got no control over them ain't no sense in worrying."

# "If my uniform doesn't get dirty, I haven't done anything in the baseball game."
**—Henderson**

## RICKEY HENDERSON

Rickey Henderson is the greatest leadoff hitter of all time; books could be written on his baserunning alone. He is baseball's "Man of Steal," swiping a record 1,406 bases, including 130 in 1982. Henderson played into his mid-40s with a body that looked like it was chiseled out of granite. No wonder those who saw him play high school football thought that he would end up in the Professional Football Hall of Fame in Canton instead of alongside Babe Ruth in Cooperstown. Henderson's personality matched his skills. His hot-dog style, bright wristbands and one-handed catches inspired a generation of athletes that came after him. And Rickey knew all along that he was doing something special. Yet his seemingly accidental humor often distracted from his occasional arrogance.

Former Padres General Manager Kevin Towers, between giggles, remembered Henderson complaining about his seat on the bus. Towers told Henderson he could sit wherever he wanted because of his tenure.

"Tenure? Rickey's got 15 years," Henderson said.

If Henderson didn't invent talking in the third person, he certainly perfected it. Said Henderson as he stalked Lou Brock's all-time stolen base record: "I would like to let my fingers and wrists and shoulders and knees have a year off. … But Rickey Henderson is expected to steal."

As a free agent later in his career, Henderson called Oakland General Manager Billy Beane and said, "Rickey would still like to play in the Big Leagues." Not surprisingly, his Hall of Fame induction speech was widely anticipated. He butchered a few names and thanked Charles Finley and his donkey. But Henderson would end up surprising — like he often did on the diamond. "I am now in the class of the greatest players of all time. And at this moment, I am very, very humble."

## MANNY RAMIREZ

There aren't many gray areas when it comes to Manny Ramirez. Fans, foes and teammates either love or loath him. But regardless of the conflicting views, there is no one unclear about the fact that Ramirez was one of the greatest sluggers of all time, particularly in the playoffs and the World Series. Still, for all of his career milestones, his critics have a hard time seeing beyond his penchant for puzzling behavior.

In 2005, Ramirez termed his attitude toward life as "Manny being Manny." There are so many Manny moments, they could have a Hall of Fame of their own. In his early years with the Cleveland Indians, he dyed his hair orange. He lost a paycheck in a boot. With the Red Sox, he did things that are impossible to make up. With Red Sox center fielder Johnny Damon racing to retrieve a baseball off the outfield wall, Ramirez inexplicably came in from left field and lined up as a cutoff man, leaping to cut off Damon's throw. On July 18, 2005, Ramirez ducked into the Green Monster to go to the bathroom — during a mound visit in the middle of the game. The incident became even funnier when Red Sox starter Wade Miller began to pitch just as Manny reappeared. In Baltimore during the 2008 season, he caught a ball, scaled the fence and high-fived a fan all in one motion, evidence of a player who lives in the moment.

"Pedro [Martinez], David [Ortiz] and I try to stick together," Ramirez said in 2004. "We go and have fun out there because we come from the Dominican where we didn't have nothing, so we have all this here. What's there to worry about?"

After a trade to the Dodgers in 2008, he inspired a "Mannywood" fan section filled with acolytes wearing dreadlock wigs. Ramirez turned the clenched fist that was the Dodgers' clubhouse into a wide grin in 2008. And it was Ramirez who showered *during* a 2009 playoff game. All part of Manny being Manny.

# CHAPTER 5
# GLOWER AND POWER

*In a confrontation where one combatant wields a wooden bat and the other holds a small ball composed of rubber and horsehide, one would likely put his money on the man with the lumber. But ask any hitter who had the misfortune of digging in to the batter's box against Bob Gibson if he ever felt safe or well armed, and the answer will almost certainly be negative. Certain pitchers can strike more fear with a scowl than most hitters can with a Louisville Slugger. Goose Gossage's Fu Manchu mustache and intense glare come to mind. Of course, such intimidation works both ways. Slugger Dick Allen's stare could give a pitcher hives. And although he never took the field as a player, it's impossible to forget Yankees Owner George Steinbrenner, who built a legacy of championships, confrontations and pink slips.*

## BOB GIBSON

Merely pitching atop a team's rotation does not make a pitcher an ace. Hurlers achieve such status through performance rather than scheduling. Bob Gibson gave up just three earned runs in all of July 1968. Now *that* is what defines an ace.

Gibson's ability to maul batters was numbing — particularly during his historic '68 campaign. He posted a 1.12 ERA and notched 28 complete games to go along with the NL MVP and Cy Young awards. Even in a pitching-dominant era, those numbers were mind boggling. In '68 he recorded an ERA+ — a stat that measures a pitcher's worth in relation to his peers, with 100 being average — of 258, the seventh best single-season mark in history.

But it was the manner in which he won that truly left mouths agape. There was no glitter, no smoke, no mirrors — just evil stares accompanying a fastball and a slider.

"Bob Gibson's demeanor was as menacing and terrifying as any athlete I've ever run across in any sport," said catcher Tim McCarver, a teammate of Gibson's in St. Louis.

Get a bunt single off Gibson and he might hit you with a pickoff throw. Hit a home run, and you had to be ready for a fastball under your chin. Gibson surely would have been ejected on a regular basis had he played a generation later.

As Hank Aaron once told a young Dusty Baker, "Don't dig in against Bob Gibson; he'll knock you down. Don't stare at him; he doesn't like it. If you happen to hit a home run, don't run too slow; don't run too fast. And if he hits you, don't charge the mound because he's a Golden Gloves boxer."

So good was Gibson that his dominance ended the deadball era. Following the 1968 season, the mound was lowered from 15 inches to 10 inches in large part because of Gibson. He said his pitching talent was a gift, but that undersells his hard work and athleticism. A former Harlem Globetrotter, Gibson won nine Gold Glove Awards for his superlative defense. And while he is enshrined in the Hall of Fame for his stats — 251 wins, two Cy Young Awards — hitters will forever remember his scowl.

"Winning is the most important thing in my life, after breathing. Breathing first, winning next."
—Steinbrenner

## GEORGE STEINBRENNER

George Steinbrenner, the bombastic New York Yankees owner, discarded managers in the 1970s and '80s like most New Yorkers did the daily newspaper. The son of a shipping magnate, Steinbrenner purchased the Bombers in 1973 for $10 million, saying he planned to be the Charlie Chaplin of owners — silent and unassuming.

In reality, his temperament would be so volatile that "The Boss" was lampooned regularly on the hit sitcom *Seinfeld*.

Steinbrenner meddled, fussed and used his fortune to land the biggest prizes in free agency. None of his free-agent additions was more controversial than Reggie Jackson, who fought regularly and publicly with Manager Billy Martin — who, in turn, fought with Steinbrenner.

Steinbrenner was driven by a singular goal: winning. But his pursuit of titles — he won seven World Series through 2009 — cost him in dollars and reputation. He was twice banned by baseball. Still, for all the turmoil, the Boss's legacy is secure because he brought the club back to glory.

Even harmony was no longer a stranger starting in 1996, when he hired Joe Torre, who managed New York to four titles and helped re-establish the club's mystique. As Steinbrenner's temper mellowed in old age, fans, who once jeered him out of frustration, now cheered at the sight of him. Such was the case at the 2008 All-Star Game and when the Yankees won their 27th championship in 2009, a title that was dedicated to Steinbrenner.

## GOOSE GOSSAGE

If Hall of Fame relief pitcher Richard "Goose" Gossage hadn't existed, a writer surely would have created him. Gossage was paint-by-numbers perfect: gangly limbs, unsettling control, squinty eyes, sunken cap and a fire-breathing fastball. To batters, he was a health hazard.

"No one was more intimidating," teammate Reggie Jackson once said. "When he came in, you felt like the game was over."

And what about those who regularly faced him? "There were two guys that I faced that I kind of moved in the batter's box for — and it wasn't forward," said 1979 AL MVP Don Baylor. "Nolan [Ryan] was one, and Goose was the other."

Gossage averaged a strikeout per frame from 1977–83, all while working as his own set-up man. What made him a fan favorite — and even more so after he retired — was his outspokenness. He was a baseball traditionalist, practically blowing a blood vessel over frequent umpire warnings, batters' armor and small ballparks.

"Why don't they just put the ball on a tee for the hitters? They have every other advantage," Gossage said. "You don't see enough pitchers throw inside anymore. If a guy was diving out over the plate and showing pitchers up when I played, you'd put them on their [butt]."

Surprisingly, Gossage's off-field demeanor could not have been more different from his fiery persona between the lines. Teammates considered him a teddy bear, and Gossage admitted that his salty mound act was concocted to combat nerves.

"At the end of his career, I'm in Oakland and he [joins the team]," said catcher Jamie Quirk. "After about three days, I realize he is the greatest guy in the world. I go, 'Goose, if I had known what a nice guy you were for all of those years, I never would have been afraid to hit off of you.'"

## DICK ALLEN

Dick Allen wasn't built like everyone else, and definitely didn't act like anyone else. And he didn't care what his bosses thought about it. His non-conformity made him a target of the press and fans. A malcontent, Allen sometimes expressed frustration through messages in the infield dirt and wore a batting helmet in the field to protect himself against fan debris. Baseball's bad boy was pictured on the cover of a 1972 issue of *Sports Illustrated* smoking a cigarette and juggling in the dugout. He wrote a request to be traded, and when commissioner Bowie Kuhn ordered him to stop, he scratched "Why?," "No" and "Mom" in the dirt.

He likely wouldn't have lasted 15 years if he hadn't been a fantastic slugger. Allen seemed to have too much talent to be on so many teams — five in all. He found comfort, if only briefly, with the 1972 White Sox, winning MVP honors after belting 37 home runs. He swung a mammoth 42-ounce bat, which looked more like Bam Bam's club on *The Flintstones*. It was in Chicago that he befriended pitcher Goose Gossage and began exhibiting a knowledge of the game that portended his becoming a coach within the Philadelphia Phillies' Minor League system after he retired.

"I learned so much from him," Gossage said. "Talking with him, he taught me how to see the game from a hitter's point of view, what *they* were looking for."

Allen's problems were partly a product of the times — racism and politics weighed on many African-American players — and partly self-inflicted. He was often tardy and seemed to have a nonchalant attitude toward the game. He once said that he didn't want to play on AstroTurf because a horse couldn't eat it. But his image softened with time. As the Phillies became dominant in the late 2000s, Allen appeared at a 2009 playoff game and received a loud ovation.

"Your body is just like a bar of soap. It gradually wears down from repeated use."
—Allen

## J.R. RICHARD

The story of J.R. Richard is one of dominance, guilt and misfortune. It's a drama fit for a Broadway stage that played out in the heart of Texas. From 1976 until deep into the 1980 season, Richard was the game's most intimidating right-handed starter. He won 84 games in that span, and twice topped 300 strikeouts in a single season. Pittsburgh Pirates Hall of Famer Willie Stargell predicted this run in 1975, saying: "I'll tell you what — when that Richard gets his stuff together, I hope that I am a designated hitter somewhere in that other league. He throws so hard he could start a forest fire."

Richard stood 6 feet, 8 inches and weighed roughly 240 pounds. He had a high leg kick and threw a fastball and a slider. He would release the ball so close to a hitter that "they could smell his breath," pitcher Jim Kaat said.

Richard's brush with immortality is soaked in sadness. On July 30, 1980, he suffered a very serious stroke at the Astrodome while playing catch, temporarily paralyzing the left side of his body. He never pitched in the Majors again, finishing with 107 wins and a 3.15 ERA in 238 games. Prior to the stroke, his toughness and commitment had been repeatedly questioned when he complained of a tired arm. He didn't help matters by saying the treatment for the injury was 30 days of fishing. Many teammates, team personnel and writers were left to apologize after Richard nearly died of a problem that has since afflicted some modern-day pitchers, including Aaron Cook and Kip Wells.

A Big League comeback became impossible when Richard's depth perception never returned, leaving him unable to field his position. With Richard's livelihood taken from him, his life spiraled out of control, leading to two divorces and a period of homelessness. He eventually got his life back on track, becoming a minister in Houston.

# THINKING OUTSIDE THE BATTER'S BOX

*It's hard enough to make a lasting impact on the game of baseball with a bat or a ball. Imagine leaving a legacy without either. Some umpires, interlopers and statistical masters certainly have left their marks themselves without ever being penciled into a Big League lineup. Ron Luciano was a demonstrative umpire straight out of* The Naked Gun, *while pioneering statistician Bill James quietly changed how baseball executives value players' contributions, gleaning deeper meaning from numbers. More than 15 years after Jackie Robinson broke the color barrier, Emmett Ashford paved the way for African-Americans to serve as umpires. Perhaps most unique, Morganna "the Kissing Bandit" provided grins and controversy with trespassing smooches.*

## RON LUCIANO

With the flamboyance of Liberace and a pitbull's thirst for confrontation, Ron Luciano was popular during his 11-year stint in the American League from 1969–79. Generally umpires with this charismatic mix are loathed, but Luciano's style distinguished him from the crowd. He would pump his fists multiple times on out calls and mock shooting a gun when signaling for a strike.

His confidence shone through during arguments, the most fierce of which pitted him against Baltimore Orioles Manager Earl Weaver. The two first met when they were at the Minor League level. In their first series together, Luciano ejected Weaver four times. In the Majors, Luciano once ejected Weaver in both ends of a doubleheader. Their feud got so bad, in fact, that the AL took Luciano off Orioles games for a whole season.

In another memorable instance, former player and manager Clint Hurdle said he witnessed Luciano make a call by flipping a coin. Such off-beat humor contributed to Luciano's legacy. He went on to write five books filled with anecdotes from his days

on the diamond, among them *The Umpire Strikes Back* and *The Fall of the Roman Umpire.*

Luciano was a striking figure, a former college football player who weighed 300 pounds and stood 6 feet, 4 inches tall.

"When I started, the game was played by tough competitors on grass in graceful ballparks," Luciano recalled while considering the changes in the game. "But while I was trying to answer the daily Quiz-O-Gram on the exploding scoreboard, a revolution was taking place around me. By the time I finished, there were 10 men on each side, the game was played indoors on plastic, and I had to spend half my time watching out for a man dressed in a chicken suit who kept trying to kiss me."

> "Umpire's heaven is a place where he works third base every game. Home is where the heartache is." **–Luciano**

# THINKING OUTSIDE THE BATTER'S BOX

## BILL JAMES

Perusing the previous night's box scores over morning coffee has long been a daily ritual of baseball fans. But for one seamhead, scouring statistics led to a revolution. Bill James loved the mathematics of the game, but didn't accept that the most commonly used statistics were adequate. Spending his long hours as a night watchman at a food-packing plant in Kansas, James formulated ideas that changed the way fans and executives view baseball. With the publication of *The Bill James Baseball Abstract* in 1977, he set about establishing an objective means of valuing players. The way in which he debunked the conventional stats such as batting average, RBI and "pitchers" wins didn't go over particularly well with traditionalists.

"I love numbers, but not for themselves," James said in 1981. "I don't care for them as conclusions. I start with the game, with the things I see there or the things people say are there. And I ask: 'Is it true? Can you validate it? Can you measure it?'"

James came up with the concept of Win Shares, a way of attributing the success of the team to the individuals on it. It created a revolution with many general managers, who embraced, to varying degrees, the deeper meaning of statistics from on-base percentage and the value of outs (meaning sacrifice bunts are bad, strong defense is good).

By 2004, James, who once worked as an English teacher after his gig at the food-packing plant, was a senior adviser for the world champion Boston Red Sox.

"If you believe that a select few non-players belong in the Hall of Fame, then Bill James certainly belongs," said Jed Hoyer, an assistant GM of the Red Sox and later GM of the Padres. "The last 25 years of baseball would look a lot different if Bill James had not come around. His fingerprints are all over today's game."

## EMMETT ASHFORD

Emmett Ashford was impossible to miss. And not just because he became the first African-American umpire in the Big Leagues in 1966. With unique style, Ashford challenged the notion that the best umps were seen and not heard.

Behind the plate, Ashford was great theater. He would signal strikes with a booming voice and demonstrative hand signals. One Cleveland writer described his out signal as a karate chop combined with the pull of a train whistle.

Some hitters didn't like it, believing Ashford was showing them up. And some managers — especially as Ashford worked his way through the Minors — still didn't like the idea of a black umpire, period. But neither bigots nor batters seemed to faze Ashford. Between innings, he was known to sprint up and down the sidelines to keep loose. He interacted with the fans during games, often tipping his hat and giving goofy speeches to the crowd. Fans responded to him. Ashford's flashiness also went beyond his arm pumps and gestures, as jewelry and fancy cufflinks were staples of his wardrobe.

"He was a showman, exuberant, strong, alert, loud and expressive," said Paul Wysard, a former player in Hawaii's Winter League, of Ashford's days umping in the Pacific Coast League. "He was constantly in motion, full of nervous energy and obviously delighted to be out there in front of everybody."

It wasn't all about showing off, though. Emmett took his job extremely seriously, both as a Big League umpire and as a pioneer.

"Sure, I know I am doing something to help my race. At least I hope I am. But — and you can believe this or not — my main concern, my main responsibility is to my job," he said during his first Big League season. "If I don't call the plays right, nothing else matters. All the color and soap-boxing won't get me anywhere."

## GEORGE MORIARTY

First and foremost, George Moriarty was a player. A darn good one, too, from 1903–16. His best years came in Detroit, where he displayed a whip of an arm at third base and a penchant for stealing home. He was admired as a man whose heart was bigger than his skill. While considered a gentleman, he possessed a hard spine, willing to brawl with opponents who confronted him.

Although he would have been remembered solely for his on-field exploits, Moriarty moonlighted as a manager, poet, newspaper columnist, songwriter and umpire. Moriarty never distinguished himself as a manager, instead leaving his mark for enforcing rules and writing about them.

As an umpire, he was fierce. In 1932, he fought Chicago White Sox pitcher Milt Gaston, two teammates and their manager after they heckled him over calling a ball on a pitch they believed was a strike. It spoke to his toughness when one writer joked that Moriarty was showing his age since he would usually brawl with

Moriarty
(center)

an entire team. Moriarty kept his job after the incident because few could umpire so well.

He finished his career scouting for the Tigers. When he died in 1964, *The Sporting News*' headline read: "Battling Moriarty — The Ump Who Loved to Fight." Moriarty summed up his legacy in a poem, "And so the fates are seldom wrong, no matter how they twist and wind, It's you and I who make our fates, we open up or close the gates on the Road Ahead or the Road Behind."

## MORGANNA 'THE KISSING BANDIT'

Other than winning a World Series, the ultimate goal for any Major League player is to get a bust in Cooperstown. Morganna "the Kissing Bandit" had what late-night talk show hosts might describe as a Cooperstown-worthy bust of her own. The buxom blonde interloper made a name for herself by storming baseball fields and kissing players during the 1970s.

Armed with a disarming smile, Morganna Roberts grew up in Kentucky, and the former exotic dancer's life changed forever in 1971 when, on a dare, she galloped onto the field at Riverfront Stadium and planted a kiss on a stunned Pete Rose. In a time before heavy security at the ballpark, Morganna would make a habit of racing from a front-row seat in a tight-fitting shirt and shiny gym shorts to kiss players like Fernando Valenzuela, George Brett, Steve Garvey and Cal Ripken Jr.

One of her most memorable smooches came not on the field, but in the courtroom, as she explained why she kissed Nolan Ryan and Dickie Thon. Morganna used a successful gravity defense during her 1985 trial, asking, "Who's going to argue with Isaac Newton?" She claimed that her weight was so unevenly distributed that it forced her to topple onto the Astrodome turf. Morganna parlayed her notoriety into appearances on *The Tonight Show* and layouts in *Playboy*. She loved the attention, signing autographs with the phrase "breast wishes."

## CHAPTER 7

# THE GOOD, THE ODD, THE NUTTY

*Truly a rare breed, some baseball men had the ability to confuse, humor and infuriate — sometimes all at once — while still earning praise for their accomplishments on the field. A pair of pitchers are among the sport's most idiosyncratic oddballs: Pascual Perez was offbeat, a showboat whose nickname of "I-285" derived from the fact that he once got lost driving to a game, while hurler Dennis "Oil Can" Boyd was more likely to burn his uniform than let anyone get a word in edgewise. With a mouth almost as active as his pitches, Curt Schilling might have been able to hold his own in a conversation with Boyd, but likely would have had a hard time keeping up with Charles Finley's penchant for left-field thinking — the designated hitter, playing World Series games at night, and white cleats were all innovations the longtime owner of the Athletics brought to the sport.*

## DENNIS 'OIL CAN' BOYD

There was a car-wreck appeal when Dennis "Oil Can" Boyd pitched, because no one could be sure what he would do or say next. Boyd made his mark with the Boston Red Sox, posting 60 of his 78 career victories from 1982–89 before playing his final two seasons in Montreal and Texas.

In his native Mississippi, beer was called "oil," thus the origin of the suds-loving Boyd's nickname. Boyd also liked his jewelry. Unthinkable during the days of Christy Mathewson or even his idol Satchel Paige, Boyd took the mound adorned with necklaces and earrings. In 1988, umpires began undressing Boyd at the opposing manager's request. When it happened, Boyd occasionally melted down, like Samson without his locks.

The loquacious Boyd provided plenty of accidental, hilarious quips. When a game in Cleveland was scratched because of fog, it made total sense to Boyd, even if his explanation didn't.

"That's what you get for building a ballpark on the ocean," he said.

The right-hander could be quite a burden on a ballclub, his unique personality sometimes sabotaging him. Former Angel and 1979 American League Most Valuable Player Don Baylor, a tough-as-nails veteran who demanded respect, was acquired by Boston before the 1986 campaign to help keep "The Can" in line. That could be a tall task, though. Boyd once wasn't allowed to leave Spring Training until he returned all the overdue adult movies that he had rented. A Boston executive dubbed the episode, "The Can Film Festival." But despite Boyd's flaws, he still went 16-10 in '86, helping the Red Sox reach the World Series.

Although he last pitched in the Bigs in 1991, Boyd — who pitched in an independent league in 2009 — said that he was pining to make a comeback to the Major Leagues as he approached the age of 50.

"I have nothing to lose, and all a Major League team has to lose is 15 minutes," Boyd said. "Give me 15 minutes and I'll show I can still pitch."

## PASCUAL PEREZ

Pascual Perez's appearance alone made people notice him. He was so thin — maybe 170 pounds — that his teams could have stowed him in the overhead compartment of the airplane on road trips. The Dominican pitcher also had a flamboyant Jheri curl hairstyle that made Pedro Martinez's 2000s version seem tame by comparison.

Perez was a full-blown character on the mound, his mannerisms so exaggerated that they seemed scripted. His slow, high-arching change-up was a throwback to another era, and his between-the-legs glances at first base to check runners looked like something from another planet. Fans liked him because he was different. He shot imaginary guns in the air to punctuate strikeouts, and he liked to celebrate the final out of an inning by pounding the ball into the ground. Those kinds of actions certainly raised eyebrows among opponents, but not nearly as much as his Usain Bolt–like sprint to the dugout after an inning.

Even his nickname was different. Players jokingly referred to him as "I-285." That's because, as legend goes, Perez got lost on the interstate on the way to his first start with the Braves, arriving after the game had ended. Still, Perez had a few of his best years in Atlanta. In both 1983 and '84, he surpassed the 200-inning plateau — the only times he did that in his career — while winning a career-high 15 games in '83.

Perez, for all his physical frailty, wasn't afraid to throw at a hitter. On Aug. 12, 1984, he nailed the Padres' Alan Wiggins with the first pitch of the game. San Diego's Ed Whitson retaliated by throwing behind Perez's head in his first at-bat, igniting a brawl. The Padres kept throwing at Perez each time up, which resulted in more than a dozen ejections.

"I would think it was one of the stranger days I've ever seen," umpire John McSherry said of the brawl-marred game.

## ANDREW FREEDMAN

If a hybrid personality could be created from *The Simpsons'* industrialist Montgomery Burns and Dr. Seuss's Christmas-stealing Grinch, Andrew Freedman would undoubtedly be the result. Although open for debate given some that followed him, Freedman is arguably the most hated team owner in sports history. He certainly was the most disliked during his time as owner of the New York Giants in the late 1800s and early 1900s. During his eight years of ownership he employed 12 different managers.

When he died, Freedman didn't inspire any syrupy eulogies. *The Sporting News* remembered him this way: "He had an arbitrary disposition, a violent temper and ungovernable tongue in anger which was easily provoked, and he was disposed to the arbitrary to the point of tyranny with subordinates."

Notoriously tight with his money, Freedman famously became locked in a financial standoff with ace fireballer and future Hall of Famer Amos Rusie. From 1893–95, Rusie won 92 games, and Freedman still didn't want to pay him. So Rusie sat out for all of the 1896 season. Fellow owners paid Rusie's salary so that he would return to the game.

Freedman's time as an owner was turbulent, memorable for all the wrong reasons. It was in death that Freedman showed mysterious compassion. While no one is exactly sure how he obtained his vast wealth, Freedman bequeathed $7 million in his will to build a New York retirement home, which was established in 1924. It was reserved for wealthy New Yorkers who had fallen on hard times, and applicants were tightly screened.

"He believed that worthy habits and traditions of affluence and refinement deserve recognition and respect," his sister, Isabella, explained to *The New York Times*.

## ICHIRO SUZUKI

The most popular Japanese import since sushi, Ichiro Suzuki is mostly known for his hits, notching more than 2,000 in his first nine seasons. But many people don't know that he also possesses remarkable intelligence and wit. Flash back to the 2009 All-Star Game. Suzuki sat by his locker, talking to reporters about the difficulty of hitting .400. Then the Mariners' star was asked about something that really piqued his interest: his shiny new cleats. They appeared silver in color.

"The cleats are platinum, not silver," he corrected a reporter. "Of course they are cool. They had an image of me in their mind when they made them."

Ichiro is no stranger to memorable All-Star Game moments. His best, arguably, have come behind closed doors. Several American League players admitted that, beginning in 2001, the wispy outfielder had become the team's Knute Rockne. Each year, he would deliver a motivational pre-game speech laced with expletives in English that cracked up All-Star teammates.

"If you've never seen it, it's definitely something pretty funny," All-Star slugger Justin Morneau said. "It's hard to explain the effect it has on everyone."

Ichiro's personality is more widely appreciated in Japan, where he once had his own TV trivia show. He said with amusement, "My brain has probably worked harder in these two years [of the show] than in my entire life combined."

As Ichiro became more comfortable with the American press, he began unleashing more colorful quotes. A gem came in 2007 when he prepared to bat against another Japanese import, Boston's Daisuke Matsuzaka, for the first time in the Bigs.

"I hope he arouses the fire that's dormant in the innermost recesses of my soul," Ichiro said.

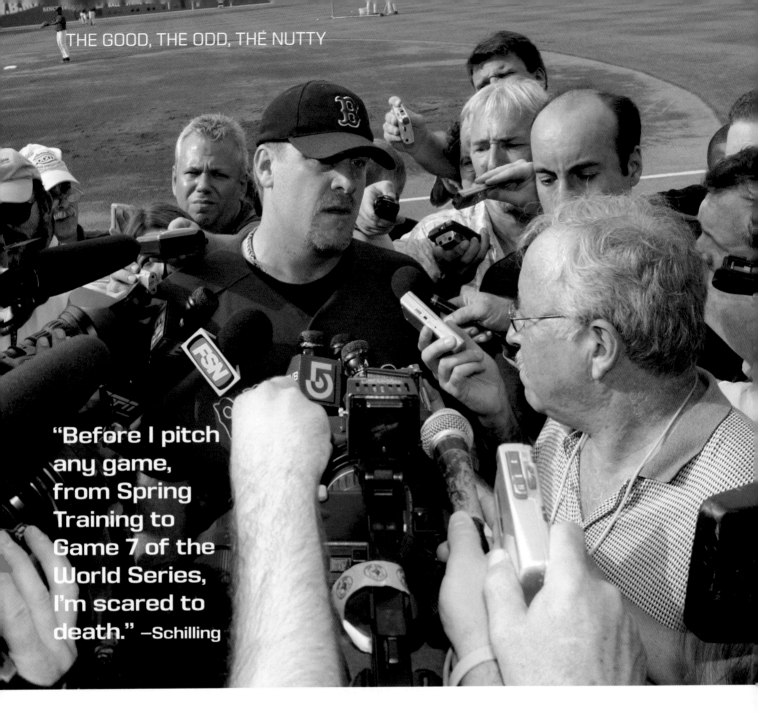

"Before I pitch any game, from Spring Training to Game 7 of the World Series, I'm scared to death." —Schilling

## CURT SCHILLING

The bloody sock Curt Schilling wore when he pitched Boston to a win in Game 6 of the 2004 ALCS against the Yankees will always be his calling card. Schilling pitched with a torn tendon sheath in his right ankle, the sutures bleeding through his sock during a dominant performance at Yankee Stadium. It was a key outing, and led to Boston's first world title since 1918. But given Schilling's penchant for savvy self-promotion, the sock raised eyebrows.

"After the game people were speculating that the sock thing was staged," Schilling said. "People still wonder. Well, the sock's in the Hall of Fame — so go test the DNA if you want."

Schilling's nickname, at times, was "Party for One." He could drive his teammates crazy with self-promotion and opinions on everything from on-field issues to politics. Former Phillies General Manager Ed Wade said of Schilling, "He's a horse on the fifth day, and a horse's [bleep] the other four." In 2006, *GQ* listed him as one of sports' 10 most hated athletes.

"I was actually talking to my wife about that because I thought maybe she had some input," Schilling joked.

While his outspoken nature hasn't always earned him friends, his play in the clutch garnered universal respect. He went 11-2 in the postseason during his career and steered the Diamondbacks to the 2001 World Series title over the Yankees. He didn't flinch when Arizona was considered overmatched. Of Yankee Stadium's stature, he said: "Mystique and Aura? Those are dancers at a nightclub."

## SAM McDOWELL

His fastball wasn't quick, nor fast. It was sudden. Thus the birth of the nickname, "Sudden Sam McDowell." The left-hander threw harder than almost anyone who has ever played the game. Yet, his name is conspicuously absent from Cooperstown. Instead, McDowell's on-field career is a shrine to unmet promise, his off-field rebound a testament to his resilience. His rise to the Big Leagues was fast, perhaps too sudden in hindsight. He made his debut in 1961 just prior to his 19th birthday. He should have been a star, but instead was star-crossed, undermined by alcohol and erratic command.

By 1964, McDowell had gained traction on the field, winning 11 games. But his personal life had become chaotic. Teammate Dick Radatz admitted that guys in the clubhouse didn't realize that McDowell's struggles with sobriety were the cause of his eccentric and provocative behavior. He showed up for 1966 Spring Training dressed like the pirate Black Bart. Cleveland Manager Birdie Tebbetts said that as long as he dominates the American League, "McDowell can wear a breech cloth and feathers if he wants." He produced plenty of strikeouts, but they didn't translate into enough victories. Later in his career, after his best season, he demanded a $100,000 salary from the Indians. That didn't go over very well and helped accelerate his trade to the San Francisco Giants in 1972. The move was a disaster for the Giants — McDowell was awful — while Gaylord Perry dominated for Cleveland.

McDowell, who finished his 15-year career with a 141-134 record, finally conquered his demons after his playing career, getting sober and helping other players along the same path. His story is widely believed to have inspired Sam Malone's character on *Cheers*.

## CHARLES O. FINLEY

Everyone has an opinion on outrageous longtime Athletics Owner Charles O. Finley. He angered and entertained with equal aplomb. After buying a stake in the Kansas City A's franchise while in his 40s, Finley became proactive with innovations to boost sagging attendance, and he continued to do the same when the team moved to Oakland. He implemented things as offbeat as neon-orange baseballs and introduced fans to the mule mascot "Charley O" and a young bat boy named Stanley Burrell, who would later be known as MC Hammer. And some of his outlandish ideas stuck, like his push for the designated hitter in the American League.

A *Los Angeles Times* article summarized Finley thusly: "He was a self-made man who worshipped his creator."

Not afraid to make full use of his influence, Finley was a contradiction. He respected his players enough to give them freedom: His dominant Oakland teams of the 1970s — which won three straight World Series — wore their hair long, grew mustaches and sported white cleats. Yet he encouraged their intra-squad tension, brawls and defiance of authority (the manager, not him). He even publicly belittled their achievements. When A's slugger Reggie Jackson won the 1973 AL MVP, Finley scoffed, "They had to give it to somebody." Finley enraged his players with cost-cutting measures, acting as a slumlord to their seedy clubhouse. At one point he even stopped furnishing stamps for the players to answer fan mail.

"Finley is so cold-blooded he ought to make anti-freeze commercials," Jackson said. "But actually he's very sensitive. When the players voice their opinions about him he is really hurt. [He would be better off] if he would just quit thinking that people are trying to take advantage of him."

Finley made enemies with baseball's top executives, trying to sell off players while constantly flirting with the idea of moving the A's from Oakland as he did from Kansas City.

## "Good stockbrokers are a dime a dozen, but good shortstops are hard to find."

### —Finley

Finley (wearing fedora)

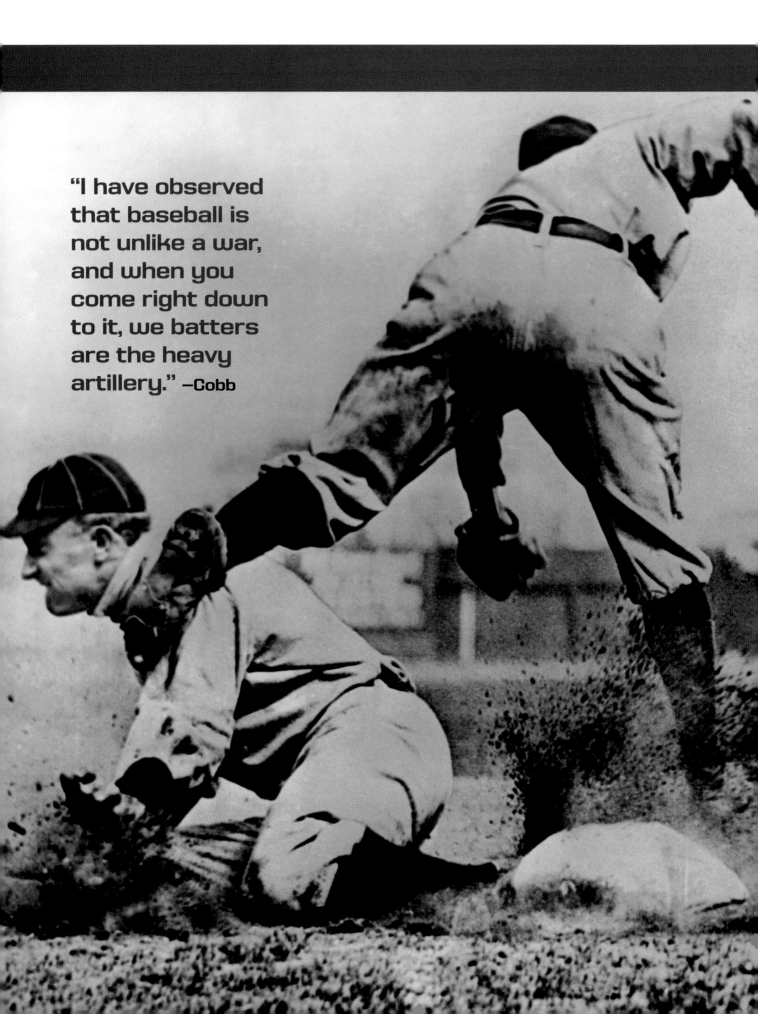

"I have observed that baseball is not unlike a war, and when you come right down to it, we batters are the heavy artillery." —Cobb

## CHAPTER 8

# OF VICE
# AND MEN

*Being a gifted ballplayer or shrewd businessman does not make one infallible. Some of baseball's most memorable characters were ultimately defined as much by their vices and flaws as their considerable talents. Hall of Famer Ty Cobb, one of the greatest players ever, was known to some as "Tyrus the Terrible," due to his fierce play and rigid views. Decades later, Dave Kingman hit towering home runs without cracking a smile. Such combinations of talent and temper are rare, but not unheard of. Hal Chase was as corrupt as he was adept at first base. Benny Kauff, a flashy player with a wardrobe to match, was banned for his involvement in a stolen-car ring.*

## TY COBB

Before Babe Ruth, Ty Cobb was considered baseball's greatest player. Cobb excelled in every aspect of the game. Using a hands-apart grip, he was the best hitter at a time when the public defined excellence by batting average. He was an excellent center fielder, and might have been the game's smartest player.

"He has no superior," said Hall of Fame pitcher Walter Johnson of Cobb, who finished with a .366 lifetime average in 24 seasons, including 22 with the Detroit Tigers.

A member of Cooperstown's first induction class, Cobb's short temper and rugged style created many enemies. He often slid with his spikes in the air and never backed down from a confrontation. He goaded opponents, and even his own teammates. Although the rivals later became friends, Cobb mocked Ruth during their playing days. Cobb epitomized the thinking man's game — he would steal and bunt if necessary. He was — in personality, education, lifestyle and technique — the opposite of Ruth.

"Cobb lived off the field as though he wished to live forever," Branch Rickey said. "He lived on the field as though it was his last day."

Many viewed Cobb as a racist, although he denied it. His views changed with age, and as Tom Stanton wrote in *Ty and The Babe*, "You wonder how differently Cobb might be regarded today had he lived another two decades." In death, Cobb's image deteriorated, and another image of him arose — that of a bitter, mean and nasty man. This much is certain: Cobb was a competitor who would do anything to win.

"He was the strangest of all our national sports idols," wrote legendary columnist Jimmy Cannon. "But not even his disagreeable character could destroy the image of his greatness as a ballplayer. Ty Cobb was the best. That seemed to be all he wanted."

Cobb (sliding)

# OF VICE AND MEN

## BENNY KAUFF

Born in 1890, Benny Kauff lived several decades too soon. He looked and acted the part of a late-21st century superstar. After two years of starring in the Federal League, he arrived in training camp with the New York Giants in 1916 looking like a character from a movie. He "wore a loudly striped silk shirt, an expensive blue suit, patent leather shoes, a full-colored overcoat and a derby hat," wrote sportswriter Trevor Graham. "He was adorned with a huge diamond stickpin, an equally huge diamond ring and a gold watch."

Kauff claimed that he could bunt balls for home runs into the shallow right-field porch at New York's Polo Grounds. After drumming up such expectations, Kauff's career was a letdown. He played just five seasons with the Giants, highlighted by a 1917 World Series appearance. Kauff's boasts that he would be better than Ty Cobb haunted him. A good player, the fans and press never let him forget his unfulfilled potential.

"While there's probably no ill feeling on [the writers' part], they have made me out a sort of swell-headed gink," Kauff said.

Kauff's imprudent judgment abbreviated a promising career. He escaped accusations of bribing players to throw games, but was eventually ensnared in a criminal case, indicted on auto-theft charges in Manhattan. He was traded to the International League during the scandal, but re-acquired by the Giants, who figured he would resume play in 1922. But Commissioner Kenesaw Mountain Landis had other ideas, refusing to reinstate Kauff even after a jury acquitted the player.

"It smelled to high heaven. ... The acquittal was one of the worst miscarriages of justice that ever came under my observation," Landis wrote, his opinion ending Kauff's playing career.

## DAVE KINGMAN

Dave Kingman had a regal name that he most certainly found fitting. Combine such a surname with his monstrous home runs, and "Kong" was a nickname that suited him perfectly. But Kingman, an imposing figure at 6 feet, 6 inches, wasn't always a hit with fans, teammates or reporters. Considered a terrific athlete while at the University of Southern California, his critics claimed he never realized his full potential. They said that his skills fit baseball, but his personality did not. He seemed bored, unwilling or unable to maintain the focus that a grueling Major League season demands.

Kingman hit 442 homers over 16 tumultuous seasons, while striking out a whopping 1,816 times. His tape-measure moments of glory were certainly memorable. On June 4, 1976, Kingman hit three home runs against the Dodgers, inspiring an expletive-laced tirade from Los Angeles Manager Tommy Lasorda. In 1979, after telling reporters that he was committed to improving his game, Kingman hit 48 home runs for the Cubs, finishing 11th in MVP voting.

It was his mix of power and personality that led to his downfall. In 1977, Kingman played for four clubs — the Mets, Padres, Angels and Yankees. In 1986, his final year in the Majors, he hit 35 home runs as a designated hitter for the Oakland Athletics. Yet no one signed him as a free agent after the season. It probably didn't help that during his final campaign, he sent a live rat to the press box for sportswriter Susan Fornoff of *The Sacramento Bee*. The rat had a tag that read: "My name is Sue." The A's fined Kingman $3,500 and threatened to release him if another incident occurred. Kingman, who didn't believe women should be in the clubhouse, wasn't remorseful.

"I've pulled practical jokes on other people and I didn't apologize to them," Kingman said.

# "I'm just like everybody else. I have two arms, two legs and 4,000 hits." —Rose

## PETE ROSE

The ultimate boy of summer, Pete Rose played the game with the abandon of a kid on a sand-lot. He was a throwback who slid headfirst into the hearts of baseball fans of two generations. He finished as the all-time hits king, and then tarnished his legacy by gambling on baseball, his legendary competitiveness providing the ending to his own Shakespearean tragedy.

Rose broke into the Majors with the Cincinnati Reds in the spring of 1963. Playing against the New York Yankees in an exhibition game, he relentlessly chased a Mickey Mantle home run that was roughly 100 feet out of his reach, reportedly spawning his famous nickname.

"Whitey Ford said, 'Did you see ol' Charlie Hustle try to catch that ball?'" Mantle recalled in Ken Burns' *Baseball* documentary. "They called him 'Charlie Hustle' from then on."

Rose played with unmatched ferocity and effort. He barreled over catcher Ray Fosse in the 1970 All-Star Game, separating Fosse's shoulder, and often sprinted to first after a walk.

"I would walk through Hell in a gasoline suit just to play baseball," Rose said.

Rose was the catalyst of the "Big Red Machine," the Cincinnati squad that won World Series crowns in 1975 and '76. He later helped the Philadelphia Phillies to the 1980 title, playing with the same gusto that made him a popular pitchman. Said Reds Manager Sparky Anderson, "Peter is baseball. He's the best thing to happen to the game since, well, the game."

Rose's addictive personality led to his demise when his competitiveness mixed with gambling as the Reds' player-manager. Commissioner A. Bartlett Giamatti banned him from the game for life in 1989. Rose accepted the punishment, but denied the accusations. By the time he confessed 15 years later, any shot of making Cooperstown had seemingly vanished.

"Say it isn't so, Pete. Why?" wrote *Denver Post* columnist Dick Connor. "Just bid farewell to the king. Tragedies end that way."

## CHRISTIAN VON DER AHE

Long before George Steinbrenner there was Christian Von der Ahe. A German immigrant, Von der Ahe was a self-made man who ascended from grocery store clerk to owner of the St. Louis Browns. Von der Ahe bought the Browns for $1,800 in 1882, seeing them as a sound investment that would bring customers into his local saloon. Von der Ahe understood business — luring fans by making his ballpark more attractive than most — but he didn't know baseball. That minor detail didn't stop him from leaving his fingerprints all over the team.

A thick-mustachioed man with an even thicker accent, Von der Ahe's meddling went beyond expressing opinions. As J. Thomas Hetrick wrote in *Chris Von der Ahe and the St. Louis Browns*, "[Von der Ahe] fancied himself as an excellent judge of ballplayer abilities, although facts show otherwise." He was harsh in his treatment of his players, believing their gaffes made *him* look bad. He would fine them for on-field errors, and was alleged to have hired spies to track them off the field, using any compromising information uncovered to dock future pay. He fired managers with such frequency that it seemed like a hobby. He did hire Charles Comiskey, building a friendship that helped Von der Ahe stay afloat in later years.

Power corrupted and sabotaged Von der Ahe. After initially currying favor with the press, reporters turned on him. His signature — "Christ" — led *The Sporting News* to speculate that the self-aggrandizing Von der Ahe thought he was Jesus.

His problems caught up with him in 1898. Hamstrung by the combined effects of more than 50 lawsuits and the defections of his best players to other teams, Von der Ahe lost the Browns following a trial involving a fire at his ballpark.

## HAL CHASE

Simply put, Hal Chase is one of baseball's most infamous rogues. He played from 1905–19, wearing uniforms for the Highlanders, Reds and Giants, among others. He earned the nickname "Prince Hal" because of his grace in the field and his charm off it. Babe Ruth and Cy Young considered him the best first baseman they had ever seen, and in 1907 he was considered a top drawing card.

Chase, though, had demons. Gambling ruined the star, branding him as a scandalous character. It wasn't unusual to hear of a player gambling in the early 1900s, but Chase took it to extremes, even throwing games. In 1918, Reds Manager Christy Mathewson accused Chase of fixing a contest while he played for him in Cincinnati. Chase escaped a ban because Mathewson missed the trial while fighting in World War I.

In 1919, the agile first baseman hooked on with the New York Giants, whose manager, John McGraw, had a soft spot for Chase. By September he was out of the lineup. The official reason was injury. Unofficially, Chase was in trouble again, this time for bribing teammates. Shortly thereafter, the "Black Sox" Scandal rocked baseball, and Chase was named as a middleman between the Chicago White Sox players and the gamblers. He was indicted, but California, where he was then playing semi-pro ball, refused extradition. For years, Chase either denied his involvement with crooks or downplayed his role. As his life neared an end, a broke Chase, living with his sister and brother in-law in California, bore his soul regarding his ties to the Black Sox.

"I did not want to be what I then called a 'welcher.' I had been involved in all kinds of bets with players and gamblers in the past, and I felt this was no time to run out. I'd give anything if I could start all over again. I was wrong, at least in most things. My best proof is that I am flat on my back without a dime."

## VIDA BLUE

Vida Blue arrived in the Major Leagues with all the subtlety of a thunderclap. In 1971, the 21-year-old rookie created a sensation in Oakland, winning 24 games and the Cy Young and MVP awards. Two numbers about that campaign stick out: his 1.82 ERA, which was nearly two runs lower than the league average, and his 301 strikeouts. After that season, this relatively unknown kid from Louisiana was touring Vietnam with comedian Bob Hope. "I keep telling myself, don't get cocky," Blue said. "Give your services to the press and the media. Be nice to the kids; throw a baseball into the stands once in a while."

Blue threw smoke. With his high leg kick and a left-handed delivery, his dominance was eloquently explained by one hitter, who marveled, "When the ball is about to be released, Vida gives it that 'pop.'"

Blue never had a season better than 1971 — although he did start for the NL in the 1978 All-Star Game while with the Giants — and certainly not in 1972, when he held out for more money. He planned to work as a plumbing executive if the A's didn't meet his demands. When Blue finally received his contract, he reported to camp out of shape and bitter. There's a "What could have been?" to Blue's career that seems a bit unfair considering the success he did have. He won three World Series and was the first player to earn All-Star victories in both leagues.

He finished with 209 wins, but his case for Cooperstown took a huge hit in the 1980s. Teammates always remembered Blue as the life of the party. But that wasn't necessarily a good thing. He went to prison for 81 days in 1983 after pleading guilty to drug charges. Commissioner Bowie Kuhn banned him for the 1984 season before he finished his career in the Bay Area with the Giants. As he battled alcohol addiction, Blue worked in the Giants' community relations department for years, a role he loved. He eventually moved to Costa Rica, where he promoted the game in relative anonymity.

# CHAPTER 9
# PRANKSTERS

*Nobody is off limits and nothing is taboo in the underground world of the clubhouse. The grind of a Major League Baseball season can wear on players, and levity is often a breath of fresh air. Unless, of course, the smell of a burning shoe fills the dugout, which can happen at any moment with these guys leading the pranks. Moe Drabowsky did impersonations and Ryan Dempster staged elaborate punks on teammates. In 2003, Kevin Millar popularized a goofy saying — "Cowboy Up" — to help unify the Red Sox. Steve Lyons even pranked himself, pulling down his own pants after sliding safely into first base.*

## JAY JOHNSTONE

During a 20-year career that began with the Angels in 1966 and finished with the Dodgers in 1985, journeyman outfielder Jay Johnstone eventually found his niche as a bench player after re-inventing his swing, finishing his career with 102 home runs and a .267 average. But his real value came in keeping players loose, playing the court jester. Few went to such great lengths, especially as frequently as Johnstone. He even authored a book, *Temporary Insanity*, chronicling his escapades.

"Johnstone wrote a book? With what, a fire extinguisher? Shaving cream?" former Dodgers Manager Tommy Lasorda quipped. Johnstone — who also made a cameo in the comedy *Naked Gun*, striking out as a Mariner in the movie's climactic scene — followed with a second book of anecdotes, explaining, "It gave me something to do other than kill ants."

Johnstone pulled off a series of pranks, many at Lasorda's expense. During Spring Training, Lasorda woke up one morning and couldn't get out of his room. Worse, the phone line had been

cut so he couldn't call for help. Turned out Johnstone had tied a rope to Lasorda's door handle and connected it to a palm tree. Another time he imitated Lasorda, stuffing his shirt with a pillow and going to the pitcher's mound with a can of Slim Fast. Lasorda loved the pranks, and mirthfully played along, once nailing Johnstone's dress shoes to his locker.

Johnstone's humor manifested itself in many ways, including taking jabs at teammates. Of placid first baseman Steve Garvey he said, "He's the kind of guy who, for laughs, does impersonations of [Dallas Cowboys coach] Tom Landry." Johnstone also used props, like a space helmet and oversized sunglasses. And he loved duping rookies. He would sometimes leave a message at a neophyte's locker, telling him to be at a TV station for a non-existent interview.

"Jimmy Piersall once told me that as long as it's not derogatory, get your name in the paper any way you can," Johnstone said. "That's never been my goal, but I never minded all the talk about being a flake."

## RYAN DEMPSTER

As 21st-century Big Leaguers are concerned, pitcher Ryan Dempster might be the gold standard of class clowns.

"I don't know if I'm necessarily funny, but I'm always cracking jokes and playing practical jokes," said Dempster, who has worked as a starter and reliever since debuting with the Florida Marlins in 1998. "That's what I like to do — make these guys laugh, keep them loose."

Dempster is well known for his varied impersonations — including a spot-on version of longtime Cubs radio broadcaster Harry Caray — and for his encyclopedic knowledge of comedy classics like *Anchorman* and *Dumb and Dumber*.

"He can quote every line. It's unbelievable," said former teammate and fellow pitcher Glendon Rusch.

For all his quips, players still talk with reverence about his high jinks. His best came during Spring Training with the Chicago Cubs in Mesa, Ariz. Teammate Will Ohman, who liked a good gag as much as the next guy, smeared eye black on Dempster's game cap and super glued his clothes together. Dempster responded in such grand fashion that he stunned even Ohman.

With plenty of help, Dempster placed Ohman's Cadillac Escalade on cinder blocks, removing his fancy rimmed tires. The wheels were placed around the ballpark, including in the Cubs' bullpen. When Ohman walked in, one of his teammates said innocently, "Man, aren't those the same kind of tires you have on your car?" Ohman knew he had just received a lesson from the master.

"He [wouldn't] even think about getting me back," Dempster said.

## MOE DRABOWSKY

Reliever Moe Drabowsky enjoyed a 17-year career with eight different teams. He struck out 11 hitters in Game 1 of the 1966 World Series, a record for a reliever. But Drabowsky is mainly remembered as a prankster. He was famous for pulling off the "hot foot" — a classic ballpark prank in which a player lights a match and clandestinely inserts it into the victim's shoe or sets a shoelace aflame. He was also known for giving shaving cream facials, as well as more elaborate schemes. His best gags involved impersonations and telecommunications. Sometimes he would order takeout food on the bullpen phone or crank call the other team. But his favorite such call occurred when he was playing against the Kansas City Athletics in the mid-1960s.

"I had pitched there for a few years so I was familiar with the phone system. I knew the extension of the Kansas City bullpen and you could dial it direct from the visitor's bullpen," Drabowsky recalled. "One game, Jim Nash of the Athletics is cruising against us in about the fifth inning. So I call their bullpen and shout, 'Get [Lew] Krausse up' and hang up. You should have seen them scramble, trying to get him warmed up. It was really funny."

Drabowsky provided laughs by putting sneezing powder in the air conditioning system of the opponent's clubhouse or goldfish in the team's water cooler. He also put snakes in everything from shaving kits to bread baskets, terrifying teammates. And one of his best tricks was throwing a stink bomb and then a cherry bomb at the Braves' mascot.

"The bullpen is right under that teepee where that Indian comes out and does a war dance whenever the Braves hit a homer," the Cardinals' Ted Sizemore said. "Drabowsky tossed a stink bomb into that teepee. The Indian went up like a rocket. I think he had to change loin cloths between innings."

## MICKEY HATCHER

After retiring in 1990, Mickey Hatcher became so well known as the hitting coach for the Angels that people forget he was once one of baseball's funniest players. Hatcher spent 12 years in the Bigs with the Twins and Dodgers. In Minnesota, Hatcher was a cult hero, but he never felt quite at home in the Metrodome.

In 1984, Hatcher was linked to "The Ball That Never Came Down." Oakland's Dave Kingman hit a high pop-up, and the ball got stuck in the Metrodome's roof. Kingman got a ground-rule double, which didn't sit well with Hatcher. So he planned a gag for when Kingman batted the next game. Hatcher jogged from first base to the mound, confusing the Twins pitcher (no teammates were in on the prank). A Twins employee dropped a ball from the rafters and Hatcher ran toward home to catch it, and tell Kingman he was out from the day before. But it didn't quite work.

"I totally missed the ball. It hit me in the you-know-where. I knocked the catcher over and nearly knocked Kingman over," Hatcher recalled. "The last words I heard from Kingman was, 'What are you doing, you idiot?' That was a thrill. I got booed by 40,000 people on that gag."

Usually Hatcher's jokes went better. He got plenty of laughs when he would show up on Family Day wearing a giant glove. He was later pictured on a baseball card with that huge hunk of leather.

With the Dodgers, Hatcher found a kindred spirit in Jay Johnstone. They conspired against Manager Tommy Lasorda, once hanging his dress pants from the flagpole during a Spring Training game.

"Those jokes came from desire. I knew those players had it, and I used them because of it," said Lasorda, noting that Hatcher hit a critical homer as Kirk Gibson's replacement in the 1988 World Series.

## KEVIN MILLAR

Kevin Millar loves to talk. Even if no one is listening. A complementary hitter on the Red Sox 2004 championship team, Millar was a motor mouth who would start a conversation with teammates during batting practice and continue it even after they had walked away.

"A lot of it is my natural personality. I have always been a little off," Millar said. "I enjoy my teammates, the clubhouse, the game. I was never the most talented player, but I always felt like I loved it the most."

Through his first 12 seasons, he hit a respectable 170 homers. Yet he's more known for a catchphrase, a walk and a prank. During the 2000s, Millar helped create a loose vibe in the Red Sox clubhouse with his goofiness. He championed the rally cry "Cowboy Up," which took on a life of its own during the 2003 playoffs, and dyed his hair before later shaving it in the name of team unity. In the midst of fighting back from a 3-games-to-none deficit in the 2004 ALCS, Millar told reporters that Boston would "shock the world." His prediction was prescient, as the Red Sox won their first World Series since 1918. And it was a key walk that Millar worked against Yankees closer Mariano Rivera in Game 4 that began the LCS-altering rally.

Millar's best trait is that he doesn't take himself too seriously. While he has played pranks, he has gladly poked fun at himself, too. In one instance Boston players were called in to a security meeting, supposedly about problems with someone exposing himself at the stadium. A video was popped in and, to everyone's surprise, the footage was of Millar singing Bruce Springsteen's "Born In the USA" back when he was in Double-A.

"It was pretty funny watching this. We're like, 'Who is that?' Then at a certain point everybody starts laughing," catcher Jason Varitek said.

## STEVE LYONS

A good nickname can be the sign of a clubhouse favorite. Steve Lyons had an original: "Psycho." Boston's Marc Sullivan gave him the name because of his fearless defense and recklessness on the bases. Psycho fit on other levels, too. Lyons did plenty of crazy things during his career, from 1985–93. He's mostly remembered for getting caught with his pants down — literally. In 1990, while with the White Sox, Lyons slid safely into first during a game in Detroit. Covered in dirt, he unbuckled and pulled his pants down to dust off, shaking his head in disbelief as fans laughed. After that incident, a fan club sprouted up, calling itself the "Psycho Ward."

"Brain cramp," Lyons said in the way of an explanation for his accidental strip tease.

A versatile player, Lyons was just as diverse a jokester. A Lyons favorite involved playing Tic-Tac-Toe in the first base dirt with the opponent. Many took part, according to Lyons.

"Only two guys wouldn't play with me: Fred McGriff and some guy with Baltimore."

Following his playing career, Lyons began working extensively in TV. He also wrote a book about baseball's wackiest moments, ranking them on his own "Psychometer."

"Hey, you're only young once, but you can be immature forever."
—Andersen

## LARRY ANDERSEN

Larry Andersen was a good reliever, compiling a 3.15 ERA over 17 seasons. Yet mention his name to many fans and three things come to mind: Jeff Bagwell, coneheads and Jell-O.

In 1990, the 37-year-old was traded from Houston to Boston for prospect Jeff Bagwell. Bagwell became a star. Anderson did not. "I had fun with it," Andersen said of his time in Boston.

Fun seemed to follow Andersen. It's rare that a bloopers film doesn't include him dressed as a "conehead," inspired by *Saturday Night Live*. His favorite prank, the "Jell-O-gate Caper," was more elaborate. While with the Mariners, he victimized Manager Rene Lachemann with this joke. In Lachemann's suite, Andersen poured eight boxes of Jell-O into the toilets and mixed it with ice.

"We also took every piece of furniture we could and crammed it into his bathroom. We took the mouthpiece out of his phone, unscrewed the lights, unplugged his clock and toilet papered his room," Andersen said. "He threatened the team with FBI, fingerprints and lie detectors."

As a Minor League coach with the Phillies, Andersen told Wayne Gomes he had been traded to Japan. Gomes became unglued when reporters asked if he liked sushi before he learned of the gag.

## CHAPTER 10

# THOSE WHO INSPIRE

*Some people are content to watch the parade pass by from the sidewalk. Others want to lead the way. Baseball has attracted its share of pioneers through the years, those who carved a path for future ballplayers. No athlete in any sport had a bigger societal impact than Jackie Robinson, who broke the color barrier when he was signed by the Dodgers' Branch Rickey in 1945. Decades earlier, John Montgomery Ward, a star in the 1800s, became the first to champion players' rights. And Rube Foster was the father of the Negro Leagues a generation before Robinson. Others, like Ron LeFlore — who went from prison to the MLB All-Star Game — inspire fans with their tales of redemption.*

## JACKIE ROBINSON

The epitaph on Jackie Robinson's headstone succinctly summarizes his ethos. It reads: "A life is not important except in the impact it has on other lives."

Robinson integrated baseball when he joined the Brooklyn Dodgers in 1947, becoming the first African-American player in the Majors since the 1800s. A talented athlete, he lettered in four sports at UCLA and was a second lieutenant in the Army before entering the Negro Leagues. By Robinson's own admission, there were other African-American players who were just as good as him. But none were better suited to endure the onslaught of racial taunts.

"He meant everything to the black ballplayer," said Elston Howard, the first African-American to play for the Yankees.

As a player, Robinson was a star, a fact that can be overlooked because of his enormous cultural impact. Elected to the Hall of Fame, he hit .311 with 197 stolen bases — 19 of which were of home plate — before his Big League career ended in 1956. Major League Baseball universally retired his No. 42 in 1997.

Following his retirement from Major League Baseball, Robinson publicly expressed his desire to see an African-American manager in the Bigs before he died. One year he even refused to attend an Old-Timers Day game in order to raise awareness of the issue. He also became an active voice in other important social causes, speaking out against drug addiction and urging African-Americans to become more independent.

"My only regret is that I wish Jackie was here to see this," said Frank Robinson when he became the first black manager in the Big Leagues, earning the top job with the Indians in 1975.

Jackie had died three years earlier, at the age of 53, after battling a variety of health problems. He humbly downplayed his role in baseball — but no one else does.

"Everything that we have today, he made possible," said modern Major League outfielder Juan Pierre. "I have a huge framed picture of Jackie stealing home in my house. It's the first thing I see when I walk in. He's an inspiration."

"I'm not concerned with your liking or disliking me. All I ask is that you respect me as a human being."

—Robinson

## JOHN MONTGOMERY WARD

John Montgomery Ward would not be bullied by the establishment. He began his career with the Providence Grays in 1878, and was soon a star shortstop and pitcher. During his 17-year career he set 50 Big League records. But his biggest hit came off the field, fighting for players' rights.

As stated in *Baseball's Radical for All Seasons,* Ward was an "idealist who relished the risk of improving conditions for colleagues who lacked his status and options." With a law degree from Columbia, Ward led the first revolt against owners with the formation of sports' first labor union.

That solidarity helped increase players' salaries. But, while Ward was on a barnstorming tour, owners retaliated, creating a classification system to cap income. In response, two years later Ward helped launch the short-lived Players League, which included profit sharing.

Ward's league didn't last, but the classification system was dropped. Upon retiring, he worked as an agent for several players and took pride in promoting baseball as America's pastime.

"Like our system of government," Ward said, "[baseball] is an American evolution, and while like that it has been affected by foreign associations, it is nonetheless distinctively our own."

## RUBE FOSTER

Born in 1879, Andrew "Rube" Foster quickly took to baseball. He had a reported 51 wins in his dominant first season as a pitcher with the Cuban X Giants. One victory came against ace Rube Waddell, which is how Foster received his nickname. In 1910, Foster offered a glimpse into what would eventually define his legacy. He organized the Chicago American Giants, considered one of the greatest African-American teams ever. While official stats weren't kept, the American Giants have been credited with as many as 11 championships under Foster's stewardship.

"You don't have to get three hits every day. I want one at the right time," Foster told his men.

Like Jackie Robinson, he encouraged African-Americans to be independent. In 1920, Foster created the Negro National League, the first formal Negro League. In 1930, more than 3,000 people attended his funeral, where he was eulogized as "The father of Negro League baseball."

"If the talents of Christy Mathewson, John McGraw, Ban Johnson and Judge Kenesaw Mountain Landis were combined in a body, and that body were enveloped in a black skin, the result would have to be Andrew 'Rube' Foster," wrote Robert Peterson in *Only the Ball Was White*.

## MOE BERG

Had Moe Berg's life been a movie script, it would have been rejected. Too strange, too unbelievable. Berg played 15 seasons starting in 1923. He hit .243 for his career, and he finished with just six home runs. The scouting report on Berg was always "good field, no hit." The joke was that he was fluent in 27 languages and couldn't hit in any of them.

But Berg might have been the smartest, most mysterious Big League player ever.

"During an evening's walk, Berg will point out planets, discuss politics, law, economics, music, art, literature and current events with specialists in any of these fields," wrote Arthur Sampson in *The New York Herald*.

Berg found baseball invigorating, loving the travel, free time and the people he met. As a Princeton graduate, Berg could have been anything he wanted. He pursued baseball, attending Columbia Law School in his spare time.

"He never caught in his life and then goes behind the plate like Mickey Cochrane," Casey Stengel marvelled.

Had it ended there, Berg would have been fascinating. But his secret life was even more amazing. He served as a spy for the Office of Strategic Services, a forerunner to the CIA, during World War II, and was recommended for the Medal of Freedom for intelligence obtained regarding the Germans' progress on atomic weapons.

"The information sent by Mr. Berg ... was used [for] guiding the U.S. operation in this field and in determining the pressures to be placed upon U.S. scientists for rapid progress toward the ultimate completion of the Manhattan Project," wrote Colonel Howard Dix.

Berg never strayed far from the game. Although his behavior became erratic, he spent his last days in press boxes watching baseball, reading and still protecting his secrets.

## BRANCH RICKEY

The death of Commissioner Kenesaw Mountain Landis spurred Branch Rickey's rise from pioneering baseball man to cultural trailblazer. Happy Chandler, a U.S. Senator, took over baseball's top job in 1945. Before Chandler took office, he contended that if African-Americans were fit to fight and die in war, then they should be permitted to play in the Bigs.

Rickey agreed, signing Negro Leaguer Jackie Robinson away from the Kansas City Monarchs. In 1947, Robinson integrated baseball, the culmination of what Robinson called "the Rickey Experiment."

Rickey was already considered an innovator for creating tryout camps while with the Cardinals that spawned today's multi-layered farm systems. And he had an eye for talent. Every aspect of Robinson's becoming a Dodger was planned. Before his signing, Rickey had scouts secretly scouring Latin America and the Negro Leagues for the first player to break the color barrier.

"Number one: The man we finally chose had to be right *off* the field," Rickey said. "Number two: He had to be right *on* the field. Number three: The reaction of his own race had to be right. Number four: The reaction of the press and public had to be right. Number five: We had to have a place to put him. Number six: The reaction of his fellow players had to be right."

Rickey built winning teams in St. Louis and Brooklyn, while later laying the foundation for the 1960 world champion Pirates. He sold his share of the Dodgers for slightly more than $1 million in the early 1950s, but will always be connected to the franchise because of Robinson.

"Some honorary degrees have been offered because of my part," Rickey said. "I have declined them all. To accept honors for signing a superlative ballplayer to a contract? I would be ashamed!"

Rickey (right)

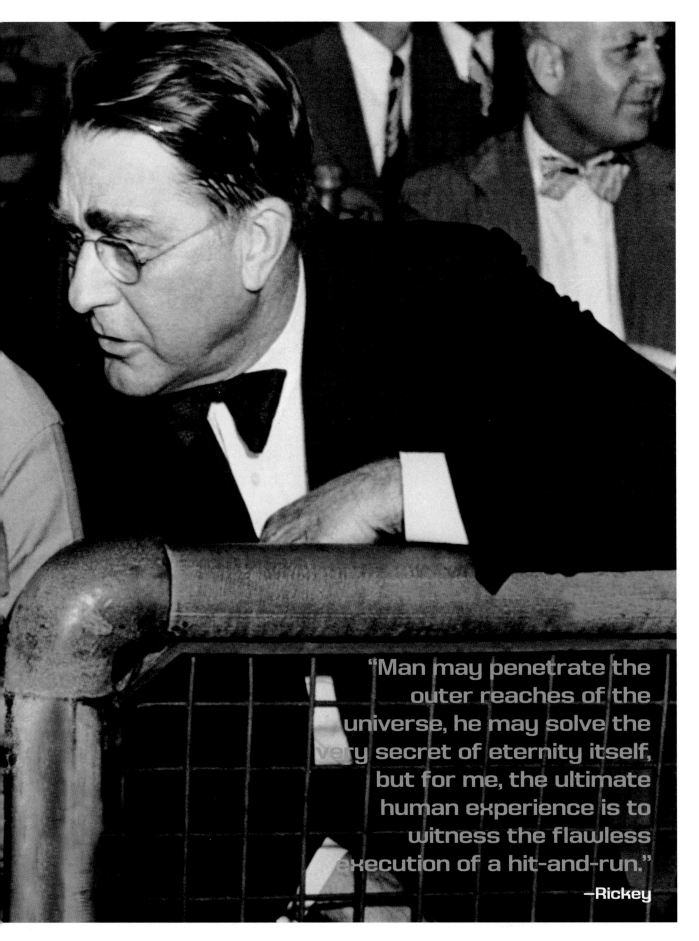

"Man may penetrate the outer reaches of the universe, he may solve the very secret of eternity itself, but for me, the ultimate human experience is to witness the flawless execution of a hit-and-run."

—Rickey

"I never want to quit playing ball. They'll have to cut this uniform off of me to get me out of it." —Campanella

## ROY CAMPANELLA

Catcher Roy Campanella downplayed his place in history, saying Jackie Robinson did the heavy lifting in breaking baseball's color barrier. But Campanella knew where he stood in the game, and beginning in 1948 he helped legitimize the African-American ballplayer. A powerful backstop, Campanella won three NL MVP Awards for the Dodgers, and in 1953 became the first catcher to hit 40 home runs in a season.

Sadly, his 10-year Hall of Fame career ended prematurely due to a car accident. Driving home from the Harlem liquor store he owned on Jan. 28, 1958, Campanella's car hit a patch of ice. The vehicle spun out of control and rolled over, leaving him partially paralyzed and confined to a wheelchair.

"He could be as bitter as anyone alive," former teammate Joe Black said. "But, no. What you'll find instead is someone sitting there smiling and talking to everyone, reaching out to people and saying, 'Don't you dare feel sorry for me.'"

The accident revealed the full measure of Campanella's character. Baseball may have been what he did, but it did not define who he was. So popular was Campanella that a benefit game held at the Los Angeles Coliseum on May 7, 1959, attracted a record crowd of 93,103 fans and raised roughly $75,000 for the catcher's medical bills.

Campanella, who honed his craft in the Negro Leagues before signing on with the Dodgers, became an ambassador for the game in retirement. He was a regular at the ballpark, working in community relations for the Dodgers. Despite having to battle several illnesses, Campanella visited hospitals and attended so many Hall of Fame induction ceremonies that he was considered a de facto mayor of Cooperstown.

"He's the toughest S.O.B. I've ever known," Dodgers pitcher Don Newcombe said.

## RON LeFLORE

At an age when most aspiring Big Leaguers are learning how to steal bases, Ron LeFlore's first heist was an A&P food store, netting him $1,500. Just 17 years old, the high school dropout also helped rob a check-cashing store of $35,000. Eventually police caught the troubled Detroit native, and he began serving time in the Michigan state prison on a 5- to 15-year sentence. Incarcerated, bored and fearing a third stay in solitary confinement, LeFlore began playing baseball, excelling against his fellow inmates.

One of LeFlore's fellow inmates was so impressed by LeFlore's performances on the field that he relayed the prisoner's exploits to a friend of Detroit Tigers Manager Billy Martin, who arranged a one-day release for a tryout. The Tigers signed him to a free-agent contract in 1973, creating a program that met the conditions of his parole. After playing with murderers and violent offenders, the 26-year-old rookie was stealing bases and hanging out with well-known sluggers.

"Prison really frightened me," LeFlore said. "I never imagined I would be in this position, playing professional baseball in my hometown. It's a terrific feeling, like I have been given a new lease on life."

LeFlore, athletic and muscular, displayed rare speed. He swiped 455 bases in his relatively brief nine-season career, including a career-high and league-leading 97 in 1980 with the Montreal Expos. The outfielder played from 1974–82, hitting .288 with a .342 on-base percentage, remarkable for a man who didn't pick up the game until he was nearly 20 years old. He even received MVP votes in four seasons, including 1976, the year he made his lone All-Star appearance.

So unique was LeFlore's fall and rise, a book and movie titled *One in a Million* were made about his remarkable journey to the Big Leagues.

## AL SPALDING

Al Spalding was a man of firsts. As a player, he was the game's first great pitcher and one of the first stars to wear a glove in the field. He played for seven seasons, going 252-65. Starring from 1871–77, he pitched in 61 of 66 games for the 1876 Chicago White Stockings, an early incarnation of the Cubs, posting a 47-12 record.

But Spalding is known more for his big-picture thinking, and was one of the sport's premier entrepreneurs during its days of infancy. After retiring from his playing days in 1877, he published *The Spalding Baseball Guide* — which is still considered the official source of the game's early history. It was at Spalding's urging that the National League constitution banned drinking and gambling. He shrewdly also wrote that baseball must use the Spalding ball made in the Chicago sporting goods store founded by him and his younger brother. Spalding baseballs were used in the Major Leagues until 1976.

Spalding used a glove, improved the baseball … next goal? Conquer the world. After the 1888 season, Spalding took his White Stockings and a team of All-Americans around the globe to popularize the sport. The team stopped in Australia, Egypt and England. Upon his arrival back in the United States, Spalding received a hero's welcome. Henry Chadwick, one of baseball's forefathers, called Spalding's venture "the greatest event in the modern history of sports."

After retiring, Spalding led a commission that wrongly concluded that baseball was uniquely American. Still, his passion and vision made him a pioneer, earning him election into the Hall of Fame in 1939.

"Spalding's face is that of a Greek hero, his manner that of a Church of England Bishop, and he's the father of the greatest sport the world has ever known," wrote *The New York Times*.

# CHAPTER 11
# SOUNDS OF THE GAME

*The crack of the bat. The crunch of peanut shells underfoot. The roar of the crowd. The play-by-play call of a big home run. Baseball is a sport woven together by familiar sounds and well-told stories. Those who have given the sport a voice have nurtured a love of the game in generations of fans. Some are announcers, and some are ex-players. All are opinionated, brash and funny, and they can't get enough of the game: Harry Caray, Bob Uecker, Phil Rizzuto and Jerry Coleman. Sportswriter Ring Lardner spread the joy in the game through prose, sharing the language of baseball with a national audience. Some of the funniest and sharpest words come from the dugout, with managers like Ozzie Guillen and Leo Durocher catching even their players off guard with their candor. And then there is Yogi Berra, whose "Yogi-isms" ooze unintentional humor and intelligence.*

## HARRY CARAY

With his huge glasses, funny opinions and tendency to mispronounce names (Hector Vee-uh-nwavee ring a bell?), Harry Caray's larger-than-life personality entertained fans for more than 50 years while broadcasting games for the Cardinals, White Sox, A's and Cubs. From his debut on KMOX in St. Louis in 1945, his enthusiastic style was unique, and he delighted fans with his trademark "Holy Cow!" exclamation of astonishment. Caray's passion was that of a fan, not a paid puppet. So when the team was great, he was over-the-top in his praise; when the team stunk, he let the players have it.

"When I'm at the ballpark broadcasting a game, I'm the eyes and ears for that fan at home," Caray wrote in his autobiography, *Holy Cow*. "If I'm such a homer why hasn't there been another announcer in America whose job has been on the line so often?"

Caray began his career with the Cardinals, adding flavor to broadcasts that he said were previously as boring "as morning crop reports." After stops with the White Sox and Oakland A's, Caray found fame with the Cubs, becoming more popular than most of the players. He was the life of the party, whether it was arriving at the team's Spring Training facility on his golf cart with a cold beer in hand or mingling with fans in his unofficial role as "Mayor of Rush Street."

Later in his career, he became such a well-known figure that he was frequently imitated by players such as Will Ohman and Ryan Dempster, and actors like Will Ferrell, who would occasionally do an impression of Caray on *Saturday Night Live*.

"Harry was a man that certainly celebrated life," said Steve Stone, a longtime partner on Cubs broadcasts. "He squeezed every iota out of the 80-some years that he had."

## LEO DUROCHER

Leo Durocher burned to win, his competitive desire almost unhealthy. He played 17 years in the Major Leagues, beginning in 1925 with the New York Yankees. He then found a home with the St. Louis Cardinals' "Gashouse Gang" in the 1930s, his brash personality and good fielding meshing well with that offbeat club. He would later have a successful second career as a manager, during which time he guided four teams, most notably the Brooklyn Dodgers and rival New York Giants. A disagreeable sort, Durocher was nicknamed "The Lip" for his baiting of umpires and opponents.

Durocher is famous for this quote about the New York Giants, which has become part of everyday American vernacular: "Nice guys finish last." In truth the quote was actually something along the lines of nice guys finish seventh. Either way, it has taken on a life of its own.

Along the way, Durocher made many enemies and didn't hide from controversy. He was suspended for the 1947 season for consorting with gamblers, and shocked the Flatbush faithful by taking over the crosstown rival Giants in 1948 in what *The New York Times* described as "perhaps the most amazing managerial shake-up that the Major Leagues have ever experienced." In 1951, his Giants erased a 13.5-game deficit to win the National League pennant on Bobby Thomson's dramatic "Shot Heard 'Round the World."

In the 1960s and '70s, the abrasive Durocher managed the Cubs and Astros and worked periodically as a broadcaster. He was elected to the National Baseball Hall of Fame in 1994, his crowning achievement being the Giants' 1954 championship in a World Series that featured Willie Mays' over-the-shoulder catch against Vic Wertz.

"That was routine — routine for Willie Mays," Durocher said.

## OZZIE GUILLEN

Whatever Ozzie Guillen thinks, he says. Prior to Game 4 of the 2005 World Series, with his White Sox on the verge of clinching against the Astros, Guillen talked with reporters until the groundskeepers asked him to leave the field so they could get it ready for the game. One minute he might praise controversial Venezuelan president Hugo Chavez, and the next he could be deriding rule changes in the game. In 2006, he called Alex Rodriguez a hypocrite, claiming he waffled over his choice of country in the World Baseball Classic.

"He says some absolutely crazy stuff," said outfielder Scott Podsednik.

A lot of people have strong opinions, but few express them like the popular manager. Of the rival Cubs, who overshadow his team in popularity, he expressed loathing for Wrigley Field. "I puke every time I go there. I am just being honest." In 2009, he ripped his young players for watching college football the day after a tough loss.

"I'm very old-school," said Guillen, who was a fiery shortstop for 16 Big League seasons, including 13 with the White Sox. "I grew up that when you lose, it hurts. Respect the game. Respect your teammates. Respect people paying."

"I hope I die on the field," Guillen told reporters during Spring Training in 2009. "I hope when I walk to change the pitcher, I drop dead and that's it. I know my family would be so happy that it happened on the field. They wouldn't feel bad because that's what I've always wanted to do."

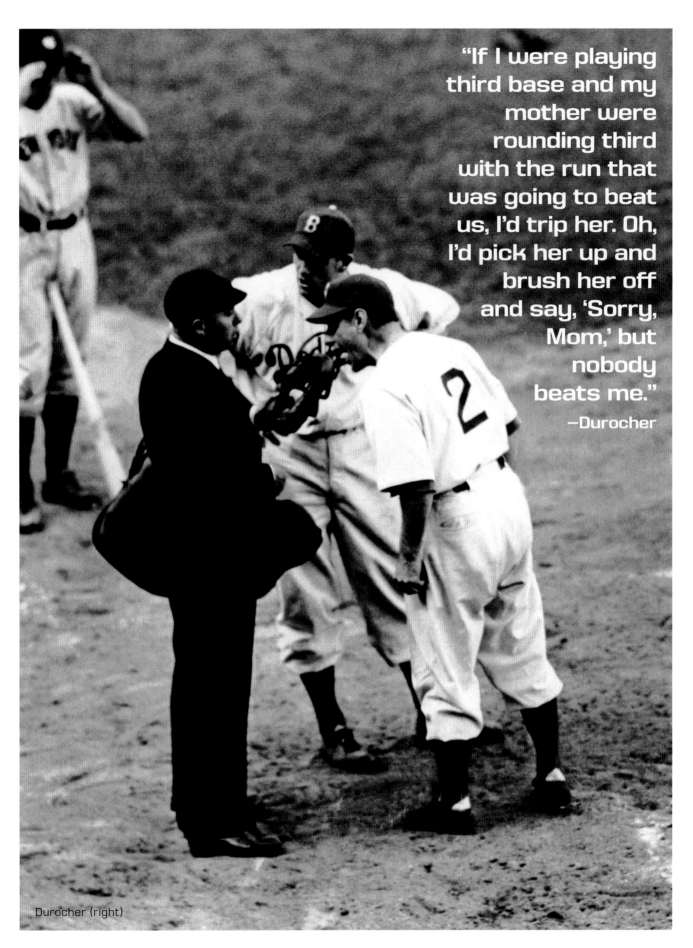

"If I were playing third base and my mother were rounding third with the run that was going to beat us, I'd trip her. Oh, I'd pick her up and brush her off and say, 'Sorry, Mom,' but nobody beats me."

—Durocher

Durocher (right)

"I like radio better than television because if you make a mistake on radio, they don't know. You can make up anything on the radio." —Rizzuto

## PHIL RIZZUTO

Holy cow, did Phil Rizzuto leave a big impact on the game! Most baseball fans under age 50 know Rizzuto as the grandfatherly figure who warmly broadcast Yankees games as if he was talking over the dinner table. Longtime Yankees Manager Joe Torre said Rizzuto "made you feel like a family member." Rizzuto, who frequently used the phrase "Holy Cow!" to describe great plays, may have been an unabashed Yankees partisan who made some mistakes in play-by-play calls — like when he called "It's outta here! It's outta here! It's NOT outta here!" after a deep fly ball. But his pleasant demeanor made him beloved by Yankees fans. He came across as the everyman by mentioning birthdays, anniversaries and telling long stories. If he missed a play he wrote "WW" in his scorebook — shorthand for "wasn't watching." A true indicator that Rizzuto had become a cultural icon, he was featured in a plot line of a *Seinfeld* episode, and provided a mock play-by-play of an amorous make-out session on pop star Meat Loaf's 1977 hit "Paradise by the Dashboard Light."

Obscured by his four-decades-long broadcast career was the fact that Rizzuto was one heck of a player. Upon his death, Yankees Owner George Steinbrenner said, "I guess heaven must have needed a shortstop." Rizzuto played 13 seasons with the Yankees, winning the MVP Award in 1950. The 5-foot-6 Rizzuto earned the nickname "Scooter" because his small legs made it look like he was motoring around the bases. Rizzuto's fire burned bright inside. He never forgot when Casey Stengel asked him to shine his shoes before a tryout. And while the Yankees' skipper loved him as a player, Rizzuto was deeply hurt when the Bombers cut him in 1956 to make room on the playoff roster for Enos Slaughter.

The Scooter had a big heart, and earned the respect of none other than Boston's Ted Williams for his rolled-up-sleeves style.

"If Rizzuto was the Red Sox shortstop we'd have won all those pennants, not the Yankees," Williams said.

## BOB UECKER

If he had been a better Major Leaguer, Bob Uecker might not have been recognized by the Hall of Fame. A backup catcher during his six seasons with the Braves, Cardinals and Phillies, Uecker finished the first act of his baseball career with a .200 average.

"Looking back at it," Uecker said when accepting the Ford C. Frick Award from the Hall of Fame for his contributions to the game as a broadcaster, "the only thing that could have screwed me up was having a good day as a player."

Uecker's comedic chops first surfaced when he served as the opening act for Don Rickles in 1969. After moving upstairs from the clubhouse to the broadcast booth in 1971, Uecker was immediately a crackup during his broadcasts of Milwaukee Brewers games.

"Anybody with ability can play in the Big Leagues. But to be able to trick people year in and year out the way I did — I think that's a greater feat," Uecker said of his playing career.

Uecker's self-deprecating humor opened up an acting career — he starred in the sitcom *Mr. Belvedere* and the film *Major League* — and made him an unforgettable voice behind the mike.

"It's his unique ability to make baseball fun for everyone that sets him apart," said former Hall of Fame president Dale Petroskey. Two phrases have made him legendary. During a beer commercial when he got kicked out of the box seats, he uttered: "Must be in the front row!" (Actually, he was being sent to the bleachers.) In *Major League*, he referred to a heinously wild pitch as "Juuuust a bit outside!" — a phrase that has been repeated countless times by broadcasters and fans.

"The biggest thrill a ballplayer can have is when your son takes after you," he said. "That happened when my Bobby was in his championship Little League game. He really showed me something. Struck out three times. Made an error that lost the game. Parents were throwing things at our car and swearing at us as we drove off. Gosh, I was proud."

## JERRY COLEMAN

There are three distinct chapters of longtime announcer Jerry Coleman's fascinating life that make him an American original, if not a hero. Of course, the modest Coleman rarely talks about two of them. He was a solid infielder for the New York Yankees for nine seasons, even making the 1950 All-Star team, but talks so little of his playing career that most forget he ever reached the Bigs.

And, if Coleman didn't draw attention to his service time in the Majors, then he practically hid his distinguished record of military service. Only when pressed, and usually in private, would he discuss his days as a Marine pilot, flying more than 100 combat missions during World War II and the Korean War.

"Jerry has told me stories about how it was in combat, what he did, but he made me promise I would never reveal any details, and I won't," said longtime broadcast partner Ted Leitner. "I said, 'Jerry, you were a hero.' And he says, 'No, the men who are buried — they were the heroes.'"

Coleman began working Padres games in 1972, entertaining listeners with a warm folksy style that earned him the Ford C. Frick Award from the Hall of Fame. His signature calls for great plays — "Oh, Doctor!" and "You Can Hang a Star On That, Baby!" — have become as synonymous with San Diego as Shamu. That Coleman never took himself seriously made both his ill-fated attempt as the Padres' manager in 1980 and his mastery of the malaprops charming over the years. He's had some real head-scratchers, including one night when listeners thought that Dave Winfield had collided with a guillotine. Said Coleman: "Winfield goes back to the wall. He hits his head on the wall and it rolls off! It's rolling all the way back to second base."

Said Coleman with a grin, "I have a lot of practice at laughing at myself."

## RING LARDNER

Ring Lardner was more wit than hit. He began as a sportswriter and evolved into a humorist, entertaining readers with satirical short stories and sketches of American life in the early 1900s. Lardner was born on March 6, 1885, in what he coined "Have A Baby Week" in Niles, Mich. While fame would follow later in life with works like *You Know Me Al* and a series of books such as *Gullible's Travels*, Lardner got his start as a sports journalist.

He bounced from South Bend to Chicago, St. Louis and Boston. He traveled with the White Sox and Cubs during the days of pitcher Mordecai "Three Finger" Brown and the fabled Tinker-to-Evers-to-Chance double-play combo. Recognized as an authority on the game, Lardner loved baseball for the "humanness of its players." They shaped his fictional character Jack Keefe, who told of his Big League experiences through *Letters to Al*.

While covering the 1919 World Series between the White Sox and Reds, Lardner was wise to the "Black Sox" scandal before it was exposed. Supposedly he boarded the White Sox train after Game 2, slightly inebriated, and sung: "I'm forever blowing ballgames. Pretty ballgames in the air. I'm forever blowing ballgames. And the gamblers treat us fair." Filmmaker John Sayles appears as Lardner in *Eight Men Out* — a film about the scandal — singing the song.

Lardner's gift went beyond sports reporting. He was a wizard with short stories and had an infallible ear for dialogue. He wrote lyrics to "Little Puff of Smoke, Good Night." White Sox star pitcher Doc White composed the music.

Lardner, though, will forever have a place in sports. As the *Los Angeles Times'* Jim Murray wrote, "He tells us more about what our sports heroes are like by fictionalizing them, not romanticizing them."

"I never said most of
the things I said."

—Berra

Berra (left)

## YOGI BERRA

Poets. Business Leaders. Presidents. Few are quoted as often as Yogi Berra, a Hall of Fame backstop with an eighth-grade education. Yet it's hard to attend a college graduation or any other event where an inspirational speech is delivered and not hear his words: "When you come to a fork in the road, take it." And how many athletes have used the expression, "It ain't over 'til it's over."

His phrases have become cliches, though some were hardly understood when he said them. Just don't ask Berra to explain how he became a cultural icon or a pitchman for everything from beer to cat food to insurance. Berra usually shakes his head at his unintentional butchering of English.

"I don't mean to be funny. I tell you the truth — them sayings come out. I don't know I say them. I really don't," said Berra.

There is often a charming redundancy at the heart of Berra's gems:

"You observe a lot by watching."

"That's Frank Robinson's style of hitting. If you can't imitate him, don't copy him."

"Did [Don Mattingly exceed expectations]? No, but he did a lot better than I thought he would."

Growing up in St. Louis, Berra was hardly a comedian. Childhood friend Joe Garagiola put it this way: "Yogi doesn't say funny things. Yogi says things funny."

Berra received his nickname from his childhood pals because he "walked like a yogi" they saw in a movie about India. Berra's malaprops and non sequiturs overshadow a brilliant career. He won three MVP Awards and played in 14 World Series for the Yankees. He was not only one of the greatest hitting catchers of all-time, but also one of the best bad-ball hitters ever.

Berra has said that he's lucky there was baseball. But columnist Jim Murray put it better: "Baseball is lucky there was Yogi."

121

## CHAPTER 12

# CHARACTERS, CLOWNS AND PRINCES

*Sometimes the drama of the game isn't enough. Baseball needs its jolts of humor and outrageous characters — Super Joe Charboneau and Bo Belinsky, for instance. Before costumed mascots like the San Diego Chicken and the Phillie Phanatic, the game's clown princes were players who might have starred in Vaudeville had they not been blessed with the talent to reach the Bigs. This tradition began with Germany Schaefer, his antics passed along to Nick Altrock, Al Schacht and ultimately to the best-known clown prince, Max Patkin. Those who didn't make people laugh made them gasp; Jackie Price boosted attendance with an array of tricks performed with baseballs and bats.*

## MAX PATKIN

Growing up in Philadelphia, Max Patkin dreamed of becoming a Big Leaguer like Athletics star Jimmie Foxx, not of earning the distinction as the game's most famous clown prince. He reached the Minor Leagues with the White Sox, but found his calling as a cut-up at Joe DiMaggio's expense. It occurred when both were in the Armed Forces, stationed in Hawaii. DiMaggio crushed a Patkin pitch for a home run, and, inexplicably, Patkin followed DiMaggio around the bases, imitating his trot.

This impromptu jog launched a comedy career that included more than 4,000 appearances in nearly every outpost that had a diamond and a sense of humor. The slapstick routine started with his outfit. Patkin wore baggy pants, a sideways cap and a uniform with a question mark on the back. Along with his trademark toothless grin, he perfected the act — mocking the signs of base coaches, spewing water like a geyser — while working for Bill Veeck's White Sox, Browns and Indians.

The routine was scripted, even corny, but as Patkin admitted, "the fans liked it." He would pretend to bat, dodging a pitch at his head and pushing over the catcher. After finally getting a hit, he would jog around the bases before getting called out at home, inciting an imaginary argument that would always result in his ejection. He took many cues from pioneer merrymaker Al Schacht. Former Minor Leaguer turned film director Ron Shelton saw Patkin in the bush leagues and cast him in *Bull Durham*.

"More people will know who I am. That feels good," Patkin said of his acting debut at age 68.

Patkin staged his last performance in 1993 in Glens Falls, N.Y, before succumbing to health problems aggravated by a life on the road.

"My wife of 24 years never saw me perform," Patkin once joked. "She thought I was an airline pilot."

## STANLEY 'FRENCHY' BORDAGARAY

Nicknamed by his mother because of his family's French descent, Stanley "Frenchy" Bordagaray spent 11 years in the Big Leagues, posting a career .283 batting average and covering a lot of ground in the outfield. Bordagaray joined the Brooklyn Dodgers in 1935, where his daffiness made him a perfect fit among "dem bums." He arrived for Spring Training in 1936 with a mustache, having grown it for a bit movie role in *The Prisoner of Shark Island*. He was the first to wear a mustache in the Big Leagues in more than two decades, and even grew a goatee during camp.

"I was making $3,000 a year playing baseball, so I figured I could at least have fun while I was not getting rich," Bordagaray said. "But after I had [the mustache] for two months, Casey [Stengel] called me into the clubhouse and said, 'If anyone's going to be a clown on this club, it's going to be me.'"

Even without the facial hair, Bordagaray's free spirit showed through in his play. He loved the spotlight, and was happy to talk to the press, win or lose.

"I accounted for all seven runs," Bordagaray quipped after the Dodgers topped the Cardinals, 4-3. "I knocked in four myself and played a Terry Moore hit into a three-run homer."

## BO BELINSKY

Bo Belinsky seemed sent from the heavens when he pitched the first no-hitter for the Angels in 1962. Belinsky won seven of his first eight starts, and became Mr. Hollywood. Although he finished the '62 season with a 10-11 record, Belinsky parlayed his newfound fame and rugged good looks into a string of high-profile relationships. He dated actresses Ann-Margaret, Tina Louise and Connie Stevens, as well as *Playboy* centerfolds Jo Collins and Mamie Van Doren.

"Our life was a circus," Van Doren said. "We were engaged on April Fool's Day and broke the engagement on Halloween. It was a wild ride, but a lot of fun."

Belinsky's love of the nightlife sabotaged his day job. He finished as a poster child for unfulfilled promise, winning just 28 games while losing 51. He was suspended in 1964 for hitting a *Los Angeles Times* writer who asked about a retirement rumor. As scout Tuffy Hashem said, "[Belinsky] had a $1 million arm and a 10-cent brain."

After stops in Houston, Pittsburgh and Cincinnati, Belinsky battled alcohol and drug problems and got divorced twice. He found sobriety in 1976 and ultimately settled in Las Vegas.

Altrock (left), Schacht

## NICK ALTROCK AND AL SCHACHT

A terrific pitcher, Nick Altrock seemed too talented to be remembered as a funnyman. He compiled an 83-75 record beginning in 1898 and was the star of the 1906 world champion White Sox, dubbed the "Hitless Wonders." He posted back-to-back 20-win seasons, then in 1912 his baseball path veered in an entirely different direction as he became known more as an entertainer than a hurler, the game's diamond jester. He first staged a mock boxing routine in 1912 with the Minor League Kansas City Blues. He recalled, "It started me as a clown, too, and for awhile I was afraid it started me toward the exits."

In 1919, he teamed with Al Schacht — who had gone 14-10 in his three seasons as a pitcher — when the pair was on the Washington coaching staff. As pitchers go, Schacht was a great comedian. The duo became notorious burlesque clowns of baseball, performing before games and between tilts of a doubleheader. It was a Vaudeville routine in cleats. They staged numerous stunts, including leading a World Series band wearing top hats. But as their popularity grew, an animosity developed between the two. Some people speculated that their fake boxing matches became increasingly real. According to Altrock, the two stopped speaking to each other in 1927.

On Nov. 19, 1934, Schacht departed for the Boston Red Sox at the height of the duo's fame. Neither Altrock nor Schacht would discuss why the partnership dissolved. Schacht provided one last laugh when he announced that he was making a comeback as a pitcher in 1943.

"The batters could autograph the balls I throw as they come up to the plate and then knock them right into the stands for the customers," Schacht said.

Despite their falling out, the pair left a legacy of laughter, inspiring the likes of Max Patkin.

"I have had plenty of ups and downs," Altrock said. "But if they took that monkey suit away from me, I don't know what I'd do."

"I got the sophomore jinx out of the way and I think I'll have my best year ever next year. There's no junior jinx is there?" –Charboneau

## JOE CHARBONEAU

In 1980, the Cleveland Indians broke camp in Spring Training with a rookie outfielder known simply as "Joe" on the roster. But this 6-foot-2, 205-pound piece of granite named Joe Charboneau was not your average neophyte. Veteran outfielder Mike Hargrove even moved to first base full time to create a spot for the kid.

Charboneau made a stirring debut in the Indians' home opener against the Toronto Blue Jays, hitting a single, double and a solo home run to fuel the crowd-pleasing 8-1 rout. He finished his debut campaign with 23 home runs and 87 RBI, while batting .289 in the heart of the batting order. He quickly became known as "Super Joe" for his exploits. Not surprisingly, he won American League Rookie of the Year honors. And he won over fans with his tough-guy antics, like opening beer bottles with his eye socket and eating cigarettes and raw eggs whole in the shell.

Cleveland's most captivating rookie since Rocky Colavito had debuted a generation earlier, Charboneau inspired a song from the Indians faithful:

"Who's the newest guy in town? Go Joe Charboneau. Turns the ballpark upside down. Go Joe Charboneau. Who's the one to keep our hopes alive? Raise your glass, let out a cheer for Cleveland's Rookie of the Year."

However, the hardest part of being an overnight sensation is dealing with the next day. Charboneau played just 70 more games in the Major Leagues after his rookie season, sabotaged by back injuries.

"It's a big business. You have to take care of yourself because nobody else will," said Charboneau after a series of surgeries. "When you're a star, they pat you on the back. When you're not, they nitpick. That's not just baseball, it's life."

## ARLIE LATHAM

Arlie Latham was a legitimate Big League ballplayer, collecting 1,836 hits and playing for four St. Louis Browns championship teams beginning in 1885. Latham was blessed with an acrobat's athleticism and was an accomplished base stealer. Unfortunately he was also cursed with iron hands — he committed 822 errors as a third baseman. Combine those mismatched skills with a pugnacious nature and mischievous grin, and baseball had one of its first colorful characters.

Latham was nicknamed "The Freshest Man on Earth" after a song that fit his ornery ways. While playing for Christian Von der Ahe's Browns, Latham took exception with an umpire's decision not to call a game due to darkness and reportedly lit candles in the dugout in protest. Once he put firecrackers under third base on the Fourth of July. And he turned baseball into soccer one day during an argument with an umpire while playing for Cincinnati — Latham and the umpire kicked his glove back and forth until they reached center field.

As a player, he somersaulted over a first baseman, reaching the bag safely. It was as a coach, though, that he really became a clown and an irritant. While working for the New York Giants, it was common for Latham to somersault or run up and down the third-base line to distract the opposing pitcher, since there were no boxes limiting the movement of coaches during baseball's infancy. The rules were changed because of him.

Latham traveled abroad during World War I to organize ballgames for soldiers. He became an ambassador of the sport in England, where he stayed for 17 years. After a stint running a Manhattan deli, Latham returned to baseball, working as a gate checker for the Giants, then eventually as a press box attendant for the Yankees and Giants.

"I do not believe," Latham said in *Complete Baseball* magazine in 1951, "that the old-timers had a thing on the ballplayers of today."

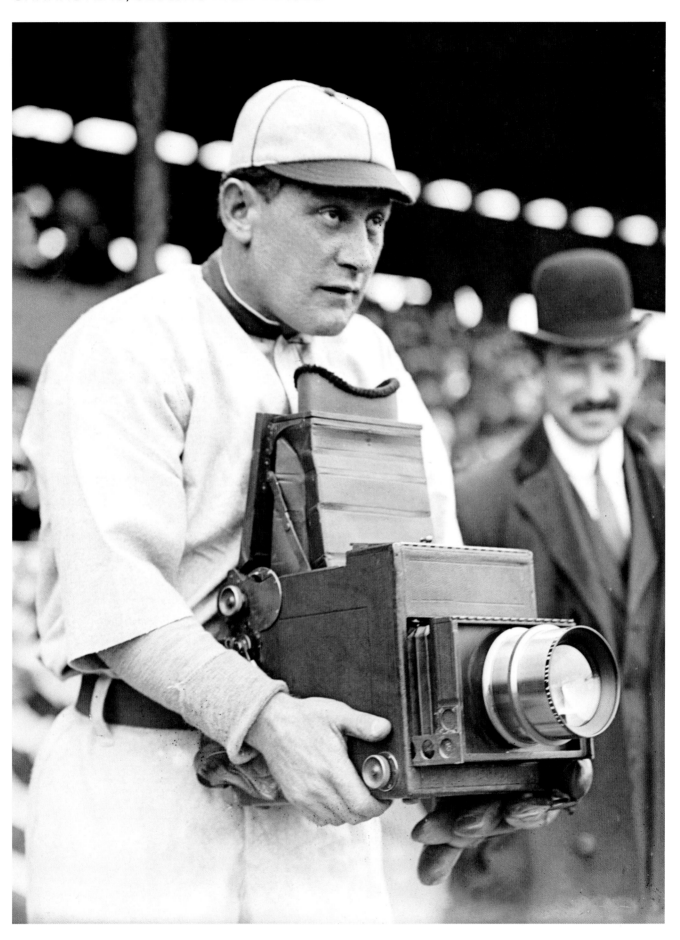

## HERMAN 'GERMANY' SCHAEFER

Following in the steps of Arlie Latham, Germany Schaefer was one of baseball's earliest madcap jokesmiths. In baseball circles, they still talk about two of his stunts — a called home run and a swipe of first base. Long before Babe Ruth supposedly called his shot in Chicago during the 1932 World Series, Schaefer pulled off the feat, made more remarkable by the fact that he was a career .257 hitter with nine home runs in 15 seasons.

On June 24, 1906, Schaefer, a son of German immigrants, pinch-hit in the ninth inning with a runner on base and his Detroit Tigers trailing by a run. According to teammate Davy Jones, Schaefer announced to the crowd: "You are now looking at Herman Schaefer, better known as 'Herman the Great,' acknowledged by one and all to be the greatest pinch-hitter in the world. I am going to hit the ball to the left-field bleachers." And he did just that, punctuated by an elaborate jog-and-slide routine around the bases.

In 1911, his quick wit and penchant for drama surfaced again while playing for Washington. With Clyde Milan on third, Schaefer stole second, trying to draw a throw that would allow Milan to scamper home. The White Sox catcher didn't bite, though. On the next pitch, Schaefer stole first. The White Sox argued that it was illegal, while Schaefer got into a rundown. The gambit almost worked, but Milan was thrown out trying to score at the plate.

His fun-loving nature made him a natural prankster as a coach, where he was the original partner for fellow funnyman Nick Altrock. Schaefer was once reprimanded for eating popcorn in the coach's box.

"Is humorous coaching of value to a team? I think so," Schaefer said. "It keeps our fellows in good spirits, and it sometimes distracts the opposing players."

## JACKIE PRICE

Jackie Price grew up dreaming of being a Big League shortstop, but was short on talent. By virtue of hard work and determination, he came up in the St. Louis Cardinals' farm system. Unfortunately, his Big League career amounted to just three hits in 13 at-bats for Bill Veeck's Cleveland Indians in 1946. Veeck knew the value of a showman, though, and kept Price around. As newspaper accounts state, Price helped breathe life into the Indians' box office.

Price was a magician, an original baseball trick artist. A favorite stunt involved the three-ball throw. He would cram three baseballs into his hand as he stood at home plate and fling them simultaneously — and accurately — to three players on the pitching mound.

The stunts became more elaborate as he polished the act, including hanging upside down and hitting a baseball 200 feet.

"I couldn't always hit it that far when I was standing right side up," he said.

Price made a living traveling endlessly from Minor League to Big League parks. In 1954, Miami Beach Flamingos business manager Joe Ryan called Price a peerless clown, noting that talent like "this does not come for free." Price was hired to boost attendance.

By 1959, Price estimated that he was driving 50,000 miles a year to ply his trade at every bandbox in the country.

"My eyes are fine, and as long as they hold out, I'll keep going. I enjoy it," Price said. "Maybe someday I will be able to control four balls in one throw."

## CHAPTER 13

# FOR THE LOVE
# OF THE GAME

*Baseball gripped these passionate players as tightly as they gripped the baseball. Their love of the game shone through with every pumped fist, diving catch and infectious smile. The childlike enthusiasm that permeated Kirby Puckett also connected him with Minnie Minoso and later with Dontrelle Willis. The desire to win and the ability to lead teammates defined Willie "Pops" Stargell. Some embraced the game, even if it made them frequent spectators — like Chico Ruiz. Tug McGraw rallied teammates and fans alike, making them laugh with his quirky take on life and sports. And nobody admired and respected the game like Buck O'Neil, the ambassador and walking encyclopedia of the Negro Leagues.*

## KIRBY PUCKETT

Standing 5 feet, 8 inches and weighing somewhere around 220 pounds, Minnesota Twins center fielder Kirby Puckett looked as immovable as a fire hydrant. Yet he played baseball with the freewheeling abandon of a fleet-footed child in the sandlot — always with a smile and at full throttle.

"You only work five hours a day in baseball, including batting practice and the game," said Puckett. "That's not so much that you can't give everything you have in that time."

Puckett grew up in an impoverished section of Chicago, but steered clear of trouble thanks to baseball. After high school he would have a brief stint at Bradley University and play community college ball before the Twins made him a first-round draft pick in 1982. Breaking into the Big Leagues in 1984, it didn't take long for Puckett to put his stamp on the game. Although his career was cut short after the 1995 season when he developed glaucoma in his right eye, Puckett earned election into the Hall of Fame, as he posted a .318 career batting average with 10 All-Star Game appearances and two World Series championships.

"There was no player I enjoyed playing against more than Kirby," Hall of Fame catcher Carlton Fisk said. "He brought such joy to the game. He elevated the play of everyone around him."

When he died of a stroke in 2006, a makeshift memorial was set up outside the Metrodome for one of the franchise's most popular all-time players. A cult figure in Minnesota, Puckett became a superstar thanks to his playoff exploits, specifically from Game 6 of the 1991 World Series. Before the game, he told reporters that he would lead the Twins to a victory. All he did that night was scale the wall to rob a home run, then hit a walk-off blast in the 11th inning.

**"I have no trouble with the 12 inches between my elbow and my palm. It's the seven inches between my ears that's bent." —McGraw**

## TUG McGRAW

Even among the oddball ranks of left-handed relief pitchers, Tug McGraw stood out. A zany southpaw, McGraw's outgoing personality often obscured a remarkable career. He helped lead the 1969 Miracle Mets to a championship while providing the identity for the Philadelphia Phillies' first-ever World Series championship in 1980.

"Tug McGraw was one of the great characters of the game of baseball," Mets teammate Tom Seaver said. "He just had a joy for life and living."

McGraw finished his 19-year career with a 3.14 ERA in 824 games, baffling batters with his "screwgie" change-up. He punctuated final outs with hard slaps of his glove onto his thigh. Born with the name Frank, his mom started calling him "Tugger" because of the aggressive way he nursed as a baby. It was fitting that the screwball was his go-to pitch, as he loved pranks and was known to have food delivered to the bullpen at Shea Stadium.

McGraw wore his sandy brown hair long, and was quick with a smile and a quip. When asked whether he preferred grass or AstroTurf, he said, "I don't know. I have never smoked AstroTurf." It was the quotable McGraw who coined the phrase "Ya Gotta Believe" for the 1973 Mets, who rallied to reach the World Series, thanks in part to McGraw's 3.87 ERA in a career-high 118.2 innings.

"He's left-handed and lighthearted and not necessarily more predictable than the screwball he throws, but he's no dummy," Red Smith wrote in *The New York Times*. Always a fan favorite, McGraw signed a plethora of autographs and wrote three children's books.

"Losing him is like losing a superhero because he's one of the most charismatic people I've ever met," said one-time Phillies pitcher Randy Wolf after a 59-year-old McGraw succumbed to brain cancer in 2004.

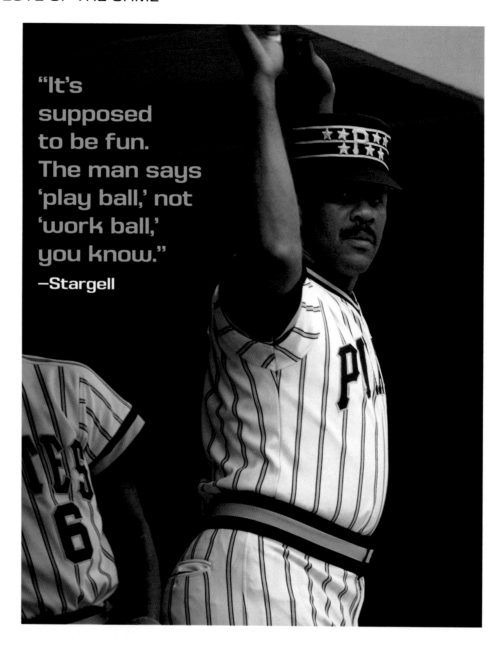

"It's supposed to be fun. The man says 'play ball,' not 'work ball,' you know."
—Stargell

## WILLIE STARGELL

Known as "Pops" because of his father-figure role in the clubhouse, Willie Stargell was a true leader. Despite having surgery on his knees in 1963 and '64, Stargell found a way to stay on the field. He played 21 seasons, all with the Pirates, rapping 475 home runs during his Hall of Fame career.

"Willie Stargell is the Pirates' man because that is Willie you see out there at 5:30 p.m. shagging flies with the lowliest of rookies," wrote Phil Musick of the *Pittsburgh Press* in 1973.

The tight-knit 1979 Pirates adopted the Sister Sledge song "We Are Family" as their personal anthem. They won the World Series that year, rallying to beat the Baltimore Orioles.

"All I ever wanted to do was win and represent the city," Stargell said.

Stargell won co-MVP honors in 1979 along with Cardinals first baseman Keith Hernandez, but teammates remember him for the gold stars he awarded them to sew on their caps in recognition of a solid contribution.

"If Willie [Stargell] asked us to jump off the Fort Pitt Bridge, we would ask him what kind of dive he wanted," said teammate Al Oliver. "That's how much respect we have for the man."

## MINNIE MINOSO

Minnie Minoso was one of those players who was hard not to like. The Cuban native's passion for the game was as apparent as his smile. He was popular among fans at all stops, most notably with the Cleveland Indians and Chicago White Sox. The trailblazing Latino star put up borderline Hall of Fame numbers during his 17-year career: .298 average, 186 home runs, 205 stolen bases.

"I am going to stay in the game as long as I can because I love the game," Minoso said in 1962 after joining the St. Louis Cardinals for his 13th season.

"As long as you swing a bat, it's okay," he said. "So I keep swinging."

Minoso became just the second player, after Nick Altrock, to appear in the Major Leagues in five different decades. He debuted in 1949, starred in the 1950s and early '60s, and then appeared as a gimmick for his beloved White Sox in 1976 and 1980. When Reds slugger Tony Perez was elected to Cooperstown in 2000, he pushed for Minoso's inclusion, but it was to no avail.

"I know that baseball fans have me in their own Hall of Fame — the one in their hearts," Minoso said after another snub in 2006.

## DONTRELLE WILLIS

When Dontrelle Willis broke into the Majors in 2003, the Marlins' rookie hurler became an overnight sensation. He had a dash of Mark Fidrych, a sprinkle of Luis Tiant and a whole lot of Williamsport, Pa. Who was this kid with the big leg kick, toothy grin and 94-mph heater? He won eight times in his first 10 starts, the most successful run before the age of 22 since Dizzy Dean, Fernando Valenzuela or Fidrych.

His appeal didn't come just from winning ballgames, but from the captivating manner in which he was doing it. When he wasn't baffling hitters with his nasty stuff, he delivered Ruthian swings at the plate, and Pete Rose–like headfirst slides on the base paths.

"I am just continuing to have fun, just like when I was in Little League," Willis said.

Willis lifted up Marlins baseball, helping the franchise shock the Yankees in the 2003 World Series. His career peaked in 2005, as the funky left-hander won 22 games. His delivery gave him a leg up, if you will, keeping hitters off balance. It was one he adopted while playing "Strikeout" in the streets of Alameda, Calif., where his mother, Joyce Harris, a proud iron worker, raised him.

"There's really nothing wrong with his delivery, as complex as it is," former Marlins pitching coach Mark Wiley said.

The problem was repeating the motion, especially after Willis's body filled out. In ensuing years, command issues, mechanical problems and later an anxiety disorder tempered his joy.

"I am not a conventional guy. I've never been a conventional guy," Willis said. "I am not worried about it. I just have to continue to get a chance to go out there and be able to overcome it."

O'Neil

## CHICO RUIZ

As the 1964 Phillies were free-falling toward one of the greatest late-season collapses in Big League history, fans in Philadelphia lamented, "Why did Chico go?" Playing for the Reds against the Phillies on Sept. 21, 1964, Chico Ruiz stole home with Frank Robinson batting. It proved to be the game's winning run, sending the league-leading Phillies into a death spiral from which they would not recover.

Ruiz carved out a career as a utilityman thanks to his versatility and personality. During eight years in the Bigs, he never got more than 311 at-bats or drove in more than 16 runs in a season. *Los Angeles Times* columnist Jim Murray referred to him in 1970 as "the only season-ticket holder with a [uniform] number." Ruiz wanted to play, but his true role was to keep players loose. Teammates joked that his motto was "Bench me or trade me."

"All my life I wanted to be a Big Leaguer and I have been one for seven years," said Ruiz, who enjoyed the distinction in 1967 of being the only player to pinch-hit for Reds Hall of Famer Johnny Bench. "I would rather sit in the Big Leagues than hit in the Minors."

Arriving in the United States from Cuba, Ruiz loved baseball and was grateful to the nation that had allowed him to live such a wonderful life. He became a U.S. citizen in 1972.

## BUCK O'NEIL

Although Buck O'Neil is not enshrined in the Hall of Fame, there's little doubt that he's one of the greatest men to grace the diamond. When O'Neil missed out on a Cooperstown call shortly before his death in 2006, he greeted the announcement with humility.

"God's been good to me. They didn't think Buck was good enough to be in the Hall of Fame. Now, if I am a Hall of Famer for you, that's all right with me," he said. "Just keep loving old Buck. Don't weep for Buck. No, man, be happy, be thankful."

O'Neil was a Negro Leagues legend. Although his career was interrupted by a two-year stint in the Navy during World War II, he was a solid player and a top-flight manager. He provided the voice for the Negro Leagues for decades, keeping memories alive with poignant stories, first gaining national attention for his appearance in Ken Burns' documentary *Baseball*. He led the Kansas City Monarchs to titles in 1953 and 1955, and he later became the first African-American coach in the Majors when the Cubs hired him in 1962. Following O'Neil's death, the Royals honored him, placing one red seat behind home plate at Kauffman Stadium — memorializing the spot where O'Neil sat for so many years. For each game, nominations are taken for community members who have made an impact and the winner gets to watch the game from that seat.

"He was a blessing for all of us. I believe that people like Buck, and Rachel Robinson, and Martin Luther King, and Mother Teresa are angels that walk on earth to give us all a greater understanding of what it means to be human," Hall of Famer Reggie Jackson said upon O'Neil's death. "I'm not sad for him. … I'm sad for us."

143

## JOE BLACK

Bitter about being overlooked by scouts and about baseball's segregation, pitcher Joe Black got so upset that he tore up pictures of the white players he idolized. The high school star from Plainfield, N.J., joined the Army, figuring he would never get his chance in the Bigs. After his tour of duty ended, he resumed his baseball career with the Baltimore Elite Giants in the Negro Leagues.

"Then when [Branch] Rickey signed Jackie [Robinson], I was 18 all over again," Black recalled while celebrating Robinson's life years later on ABC's *Good Morning America*. "I started dreaming. And that's what happened to most guys in the Negro Leagues. You forgot your age. You said, 'If Jackie makes it, I can make it.'"

In 1952, Black joined Robinson on the Dodgers, making his own mark as a 28-year-old rookie. An imposing figure at 6-foot-2 and 220 pounds, Black went 15-4 with 15 saves and a 2.15 ERA to win Rookie of the Year honors that season. He also became the first African-American pitcher to win a World Series game, beating the New York Yankees.

"The way I feel right now, it's just another ballgame," Black said the day before his surprise start. (He had worked primarily out of the bullpen that season.) "The Yankees don't awe me at all. After watching them work out, I realized they are just another ballclub. They are a good ballclub, but the Dodgers seem to be a pretty good ballclub, too."

Although he won just 15 more games over the next five seasons, Black was better prepared for retirement than most. He graduated from Morgan State, worked as a teacher and later as an executive for the Greyhound bus company. Before he died in 2002, Black also served as an official for the Baseball Assistance Team, which provides financial help for retired Big League and Negro Leagues players.

# CHAPTER 14
# LARGER THAN LIFE

*Recognizable on sight, these icons need no introduction. Every sport has its constellation of stars, but players like this could populate planets with all their fans. They stick in the memory because of their mythical feats and bombastic personalities. Reggie Jackson was nick-named Mr. October for his crowning achievement in the 1977 World Series. Mike "King" Kelly was baseball royalty in the late 1800s, while "Neon" Deion Sanders represented a new wave of star athletes nearly a century later, when image became paramount and excelling at one sport wasn't enough. And, looming over nearly everyone to ever play the game, there was Babe Ruth, arguably the most popular sports hero in American history.*

## REGGIE JACKSON

Prima donna. Arrogant. Paradox. These were just a few of the verbal Molotov cocktails lobbed at Hall of Famer Reggie Jackson during his career. He wasn't always liked, but when the left-handed slugger stepped into the batter's box, he demanded respect. Jackson's popularity peaked in 1977 with a feat that may never be matched. Playing for the Yankees in the decisive Game 6 of the World Series against the Los Angeles Dodgers, Jackson hit three home runs on three consecutive pitches against three different pitchers. No longer was he simply Reggie Jackson. He became "Mr. October."

"I didn't run from the truth. When I heard that I was fighting with the manager or something else was being said about me, I didn't mind it," Jackson said in October 2009. "It had a different effect on me. It made me want to dig deeper. I had to show people something. I loved that pressure."

Jackson put himself in the crosshairs when he went to New York after signing a five-year, $2.9 million deal in 1976. He soon had his own candy bar and called himself "the straw that stirs the drink" in an un-flattering *Sport* magazine article that pitted him against Yankees catcher Thurman Munson.

Of course, Jackson was a star before New York, an AL MVP who served as a key member of the three-peat Oakland A's in the early 1970s. A stranger to modesty, Jackson was asked in 1974 if he could top Hank Aaron's home run record. "No way. They couldn't afford to pay me to play that long," Jackson said.

Through all of his feuds and fights, Jackson always hit, stroking 563 home runs in 21 seasons.

"Richie Allen told me once, 'Don't speak with your mouth, speak with your bat,'" Jackson said. "Through [the bat], you can speak to the world."

"Fans don't boo
nobodies."

—Jackson

## MIKE 'KING' KELLY

Mike "King" Kelly provided the blueprint for future superstars. A colorful character with astonishing athletic ability, he was a terrific catcher who is credited both with creating signs to call pitches for his batterymate (even if the signal was moving tobacco in his cheeks) and the hit-and-run play. He crafted his legend with the Chicago White Stockings, hitting .354 in 1884. As a base runner, he was ahead of his time, incorporating such moves as the hook slide into his game.

He swiped 84 bases in 1887, notable because that was his first year with the Boston Beaneaters, which paid $10,000 to buy him from Chicago. In 1890, Kelly moved across town to play for the Boston Reds in the short-lived Players League.

"I am going to prove I know a thing or two about handling a team," Kelly said at the time. "My mission from today is to make this new league a success."

After signing with the Reds, Kelly received a three-year, $15,000 contract to return to the Beaneaters as captain, player and manager. Kelly turned down that offer but ultimately returned to the Beaneaters at the end of the 1891 campaign.

Fans adored Kelly's aggressive style and flocked to see him play. As stated in his 1894 obituary in *The New York Times*, his "stealing of bases won for him the expression, 'Slide, Kelly, slide!'"

His on-field antics were outrageous. Kelly once pretended to catch a long fly ball as darkness fell during a game, and hustled into the dugout before anyone realized it had gone well over his head.

Off the field he was part Michael Jackson, part Reggie Jackson. According to newspaper accounts of the day, Kelly was prone to traveling with a monkey and a Japanese valet. And his wardrobe was anything but modest. He wore leather shoes, bejeweled hats and drank as if every night was a celebration.

Hall of Famer Cap Anson said Kelly was his own worst enemy. He lived life fast and to the fullest, and he was fascinated by himself, becoming the first athlete to write an autobiography. His life was cut short in 1894 when he died from pneumonia just after he traveled to Boston to perform comedy bits for the London Gaiety Girls Theatrical Company.

## DEION SANDERS

Football pundits consider Deion Sanders one of the greatest NFL cornerbacks ever. He could shut down half the football field, rendering a receiver useless. But the one thing he would never close down was his mouth. With bravado and jewelry, the two-sport star created a persona — "Neon Deion," a.k.a. "Prime Time." The Yankees, looking to capitalize on Sanders' popularity as a football star at Florida State, drafted and signed him as an outfielder in 1988. The next year, the NFL's Atlanta Falcons also tapped Sanders, picking him fifth overall.

By 1989 he was in the Bigs. And by 1990 he was annoying the establishment and fighting with star catcher Carlton Fisk. Sanders allegedly drew a dollar sign in the batter's box before digging in against Fisk's White Sox. Then he failed to run out a pop-up, angering Fisk. During Sanders' next at-bat, the two exchanged words.

"You find a black man who isn't afraid to open his mouth, and people are going to be crawling to get stuff out of him," Sanders said.

The flamboyant Sanders' best season came in 1992, when he hit .304 with 14 triples and 26 steals for Atlanta. The Braves traded Sanders in May 1994. He played baseball off and on for seven more years as he continued to excel in the NFL.

Despite a middling baseball career, Sanders had his moments. He was the first man to play in both a World Series and a Super Bowl, and he introduced Braves fans to the Tomahawk Chop, which he brought over from Florida State. His emotional high point came with the Reds in 2001. In his return to baseball after four years of focusing solely on football, Sanders went 3 for 3 and received his first curtain call.

"I wish my vocabulary was equipped to explain it," Sanders humbly said. "I was moved — teary-eyed."

## BO JACKSON

He was a thunderbolt of athleticism and marketing. Bo Jackson wasn't just an athlete, he was an assertion: Bo Knows. Nike made that phrase famous after Jackson went from winning the 1985 Heisman Trophy as the country's top collegiate football player to simultaneously starring in the Major Leagues with the Kansas City Royals and in the NFL for the Los Angeles Raiders.

"I have to do what Bo wants to do," Jackson responded when asked about choosing between baseball and football. "I'll decide [which sport] when the time comes. Why should I think about it? I'm having fun."

It could be argued that baseball has never seen a better physical specimen than Jackson. He was 6 foot 1 and 225 pounds, and ran the 40-yard dash in 4.125 seconds. And he smacked home runs that sounded like cannon fire.

"Anything Bo sets his mind to athletically, he can get done," Hall of Famer George Brett said of his Royals teammate.

Jackson did things that left mouths agape, cracking bats over his massive thigh, running down fly balls into the gap and scaling fences like Spiderman. He regularly crushed 450-foot homers, like the laser off Giants hurler Rick Reuschel in the bottom of the first in the 1989 All-Star Game.

Jackson's legend grew when in his fifth NFL game he ran for 221 yards, embarrassing the Seahawks' top draft pick, linebacker Brian Bosworth, in the process. As a football player, he rushed for 2,782 yards on 515 carries in an abbreviated stint.

Just like that, though, his career went poof. Jackson suffered a crushing hip injury during a 1991 NFL playoff game. He would play three more seasons in the Bigs with the White Sox and Angels, the last two with an artificial hip, but he was a shell of himself.

"This is a rough way to go, but I have to accept that fact," Jackson said.

"If I'd just tried for them dinky singles, I could've batted around .600." —Ruth

## BABE RUTH

When it comes to baseball legends, even cultural legends, there's Babe Ruth — and then there's everyone else. No one approaches his popularity. He was the right man at the right time, expanding the possibilities for hitters and celebrities. He saved the sport after the 1919 "Black Sox" scandal. The Babe's powerful body twisted into the ground like a corkscrew when he swung and missed. And Ruth lived life like he swung the bat — all out, all the time. That made his failures just as dramatic as his successes.

He was so flamboyantly different — he evolved from a star left-handed pitcher for the Red Sox to a slugger for the Yankees — that he *had* to be watched. He hit 54 homers in his first year with the Yankees in 1920. By 1921, he was the sport's all-time home run leader, an honor he held until Hank Aaron eclipsed his 714 blasts in 1974.

Teams started walking him, which reporters labeled "the most unpopular play in baseball." As a player, Ruth was a walking caricature. He owned a 2.28 ERA and 94 wins in 10 seasons as a pitcher, and had no rival as a power hitter — or as a showman. People claim he even called his shot during Game 3 of the 1932 World Series at Wrigley Field, and this might-have-been moment remains one of the most celebrated acts in baseball history.

"The old gag that Waite Hoyt used was, 'All the lies about Ruth are true,'" author Robert Creamer wrote. "Ruth accrued legends."

When he wasn't dedicating homers to sick children, he was getting suspended for barnstorming with Negro Leaguers and missing time for carousing. His passing in 1948 was international news, and the world mourned him like a fallen head of state.

"Babe Ruth had all the qualities of a hero, and as an exemplar of clean sport was an inspiration to tens of thousands of rooters of all ages," said President Harry Truman.

# SOURCE NOTES

## CHAPTER 1

9. "Mark Fidrych's explanation of his mound antics." YouTube, Stone, Steve, Mengelt, John and Brickhouse, Jack. "Once a Star," MediaBurnArchive. 14 Feb. 2007.

9. "Al Kaline talking about Mark Fidrych's impact." Torre, Palbo. "Right Up Till The End, Mark Fidrych Was Living the Dream." Published at sportsillustrated.com. 15 April 2009.

11. "Luis Tiant on his eccentric pitching delivery." Cope, Myron. "Where There's Smoke, There's Luis." *Sports Illustrated*. 7 May 1973.

11. "Luis Tiant elaborates on his pitching motion." Dolgan, Bob. "When the Tribe's Luis Tiant threw four consecutive shutouts." *Baseball Digest*. 1 July 2002.

11. "Dizzy Dean on his bravado." Okrent, Daniel. *Baseball Anecdotes*. 1989.

11. "Dizzy Dean passes away." Murray, Jim. *Los Angeles Times*. 19 July 1974.

13. "Bert Blyleven on disappearing cut-ups." Schmitz, Brian. "Flakes: Clubhouse comics becoming vanishing breed among gloom and doom." *Beaver County Times*. 22 April 1986.

14. "Roger McDowell as the Second Spitter." "The Boyfriend," Season 3, Episodes 17, 18 *Seinfeld*. 12 Feb. 1992.

14. "Roger McDowell about Pranks." Cooper, Jon. "Pranks for The Memories." *Village Voice*. 22 July 2003.

16. "Dan Quisenberry on a memorable game." Quisenberry, Dan. "The Game I'll Never Forget." *Baseball Digest*. Sept. 1989.

16. "Dan Quisenberry on backs against the wall." Goldstein, Richard. "Dan Quisenberry, 45, Submarine-Style pitcher." *The New York Times*. 1 Oct. 1998.

18. "Billy Loes as a reclamation project." Harwell, Ernie. "Richards' Deluxe Retreads." *Baseball Digest*. Sept. 1957.

19. "A look back at Mike Marshall's career." Macht, L. Norman. "Remembering The Days of former pitcher Mike Marshall." *Baseball Digest*. Dec. 2003.

19. "About Mike Marshall's back injury." Vass, George. "Tommy John: The Pitcher with the bionic arm." *Baseball Digest*. Sept. 1979.

19. "Andy Messersmith on Mike Marshall's durability." Fimrite, Ron. "He Also Serves Who Sits and Waits." *Sports Illustrated*. 12 Aug. 1974.

21. "Background on Satchel Paige." "Satchel Paige, Negro Ballplayer, is one of the best pitchers in the Game." *LIFE*. 2 June 1941.

21. "Wit of Satchel Paige." *Satchel Sez: The Wit, Wisdom and World of Leroy 'Satchel' Paige*. Sterry, David; Eckstut, Arielle. New York: Three Rivers Press, 2001.

## CHAPTER 2

22. "Bill Lee on American Society." Lee, William. Lally, Richard. *Wrong Stuff*. New York: Penguin Books, 1984.

24. "Fritz Peterson looking back on his career." LaPointe, Joe. "In His Book, Fritz Peterson Discusses Pranks, Teammates and Swapping Wives." *The New York Times*. 17 Sept. 2009.

24. "Marriage switch sours quickly." "The Sexes: Switch Pitchers." *TIME*. 19 March 1973.

24. "Fritz Peterson's pranks." Wulf, Steve. "Sparky Lyle MVP, That's Most Valuable Prankster." *Baseball Digest*. July 1977.

26. "Background on Al Hrabosky." Edes, Gordon. "Remembering The Mad Hungarian." *Baseball Digest*. August 2003.

27. "Captain Quirk: Yoga, Love Beads and Leisure Suite: Say Hello to the A's Ace pitcher, Barry Zito." *People Magazine*. 29 July 2002

27. "Barry Zito on hiding his personality." Urban, Mychael. KNBR San Francisco. 17 June 2008.

29. "Fernando Valenzuela creates stir." Kaplan, Jim. "Will The Bubble Ever Burst?" *Sports Illustrated*. 18 May 1991.

29. "Fernando Valenzuela's hard luck." Castro, Tony. "Something Screwy Going On Here." *Sports Illustrated*. 8 July 1985.

30. "The comedic nature of Lefty Gomez." Lewis, Jerry. "Lefty Gomez: He Enlivened The Game with his Comedy." *Baseball Digest*. Dec. 1977.

30. "Lefty Gomez's sense of humor and ability." Berkow, Ira. "Sports of The Times: Lefty Gomez Was Hard To Beat." *The New York Times*. 20 Feb. 1989.

## CHAPTER 3

32. "Casey Stengel on the 1962 Mets." Breslin, Jimmy. "The Worst Team Ever." *Sports Illustrated*. 13 Aug. 1962.

34. "Background on Bobby Valentine." Waldstein, David. "Japanese Fans Mobilize to Keep Valentine as Their Manager." *The New York Times*. 20 May 2009.

34. "Bobby Valentine on Baseball." Kepner, Tyler. "Full Transcript: Bobby Valentine Interview." *The New York Times*. 3 March 2007.

35. "The Facts behind Earl Weaver." Verducci, Tom. "A Mind for The Game." *Sports Illustrated*. 13 June 2009.

35. "Earl Weaver's rant on an umpire." Olesker, Michael. "Weaver's passion a gift to game, to Hall." *The Baltimore Sun*. 4 Aug. 1996.

37. "On Tom Lasorda's fall at the 2001 All-Star Game." "Look Out, Tommy!" Associated Press. 10 July 2001.

40. "Sparky Anderson's return to Detroit." "Sparky Saluted with Tigers' 1984 World Series Team." Associated Press. 28 Sept. 2009.

41. "Billy Martin's obituary." Chass, Murray. "Billy Martin of the Yankees Killed in Crash on Icy Road." *The New York Times*. 26 Dec. 1989.

42. "Don Zimmer's time with the Padres." Peterson, Harold. "Padres are no Longer Patsies." *Sports Illustrated*. 29 May 1972.

42. "Don Zimmer on being Joe Torre's bench coach." "He Said It." *Sports Illustrated*. 13 May 2002.

## CHAPTER 4

47. "Babe Herman on doubling into a double-play." Murray, Jim. "Herman Debunks a Famous Legend." *Baseball Digest*. Jan. 1973.

48. "Turk Wendell on his superstitions and hunting." Pauly, Brent. "Wendell Wears Respect for Hunting Proudly." Published at ESPN.com. 9 April 2002.

48. "Background on Wendell's pitching, personality." Kepner, Tyler. "Even Wendell's Fastball Zigs and Zags." *The New York Times*. 15 March 2001.

49. "About Rivers' weird ways." McKenzie, Mike. "Mickey Rivers' Views Out of Left Field." *Baseball Digest*. Feb. 1984.

50. "On Rickey Henderson's brilliance." Gammons, Peter. "Man of Steal." *Sports Illustrated*. 1 Oct. 1990.

53. "On Manny Ramirez's hitting, personality." Pierce, Charles. "A Cut Above." *Sports Illustrated*. 5 July 2004.

## CHAPTER 5

55. "The dominance of Bob Gibson and Denny McLain." Leggett, William. "Herman Debunks a Famous Legend." *Sports Illustrated*. 30 Sept. 1968.

55. "Background on Bob Gibson's greatest season." Keri, Jonah. "Forty years later, Gibson's 1.12 ERA remains a magic number." Published at ESPN.com. 7 Feb 2008.

58. "Background on Dick Allen with White Sox." Fimrite, Ron. "What's Going On Out There?" *Sports Illustrated*. 12 June 1972.

58. "The antics on Dick Allen." King, Kelley. "Dick Allen, Baseball Bad Boy." *Sports Illustrated*. 19 July 1999.

61. "About J.R. Richard's stroke." Nack, William. "Now Everyone Believes Him." *Sports Illustrated*. 18 Aug. 1980.

61. "Willie Stargell on J.R. Richard's fastball." Robinson, Frank. Silverman, Al. "The Day I Settled with Don Drysdale." *Baseball Digest*. Oct. 1975.

## CHAPTER 6

62. "On The death of Ron Luciano." Goldstein, Richard. "Ron Luciano, a Former Umpire in Big Leagues, a Suicide at 57." *The New York Times*. 20 Jan. 1995.

64. "Discovering Bill James." Okrent, Daniel. "He Does It By The Numbers." *Sports Illustrated*. 25 May 1981.

64. "Bill James with the Boston Red Sox." Edes, Gordon. "Still batting around those 'Abstract' ideas." *Boston Globe*. 12 March 2008.

64. "Background on Emmett Ashford." Falls, Joe. "Ump Gets The Decision." *Baseball Digest*. July 1966.

66. "A memorable fight for Moriarty." Merron, Jeff. "Put Up Your Dukes." Published at ESPN.com. 24 April 2003.

67. "Catching up to Morganna The Kissing Bandit." Rushin, Steve. "Where Are They Now? Morganna." *Sports Illustrated*. 23 June 2003.

## CHAPTER 7

68. "On the weirdness of Oil Can." Kurkjian, Tim. "Never a Dull Moment with 'Can' Around." Published at ESPN.com. 26 May 2005.

68. "Can talks about a comeback." Cafardo, Nick. "At 49, Boyd wants to turn fantasy into reality." *Boston Globe*. 15 Feb. 2009.

71. "A top brawl involving Pascual Perez." Merron, Jeff. "Put Up Your Dukes." Published at ESPN.com. 24 April 2003.

71. "Andrew Freedman's firing practices." Tarvin, A.H. "One for Home and One for the Road." *Baseball Digest*. July 1951.

71. "Andrew Freedman's retirement home." Gray, Christopher. "Streetscapes: The Andrew Freedman Home." *The New York Times*. 23 May 1999.

72. "Justin Morneau on Ichiro's All-Star Game speech." Passan, Jeff. "Ichiro's speech to All-Stars revealed." Published at Yahoo.com. 15 July 2008.

72. "Ichiro's sense of humor." Lefton, Brad. "Ichiro matches wits on own TV Show." *The Seattle Times*. 21 March 2007.

72. "Ichiro on facing Daisuke Matsuzaka." Sheinin, Dave. "Matsuzaka Ready to give Ichiro Taste of Home." *Washington Post*. 11 April 2007.

74. "The Indians trade of Sam McDowell." Eskridge, Neal. "Why the Indians Said Goodbye to Sudden Sam." *Baseball Digest*. March 1972.

74. "A strong year for Sam McDowell." "Baseball: Sudden Sam, the Shutout Man." *TIME*. 13 May 1966.

75. "Curt Schilling on being hated." Duerson, Adam. "They Said It." *Sports Illustrated*. 6 March 2006.

75. "Curt Schilling on the bloody sock game." Schwarz, Alan. "Schilling: I felt like something special was happening." Published at ESPN.com. 26 April 2007.

76. "The legacy of Charles O. Finley." Acocella, Nick. "ESPN SportsCentury: Charles Finley." Published at ESPN.com. 2007.

## CHAPTER 8

78. "The misunderstood nature of Ty Cobb." Stanton, Tom. *Ty and The Babe*. New York: Thomas Dunne Books, 2007.

78. "The greatness of Ty Cobb." Alexander, Charles. *Ty Cobb*. New York: Oxford University Press, 1984.

81. "Kingman sends live rat to female reporter." "Kingman Fined $3,500." Associated Press. 25 June 1986.

81. "Tommy Lasorda's rant about Dave Kingman." "Scorecard: Top 10 Most Embarrassing TV/ Radio Interview Moments." *Sports Illustrated*. 5 Aug. 2004.

81. "Background on Benny Kauff." Jones, David. "Benny Kauff." The Baseball Biography Project. Published at bioproj.sabr.org

82. "Rose busted for gambling." Connor, Dick. "Rose Epitomizes Sports Tragedy." *Denver Post*. 22 June 1989.

82. "Rose's collision with Ray Fosse." Kroichick, Ron. "Bowled Over." *San Francisco Chronicle*. 10 July 1999.

82. "Rose's love for baseball." Rose, Pete. *My Prison Without Bars*. New York: Rodale, 2004.

82. "Rose's pursuit of Ty Cobb." Reilly, Rick. "On Deck for The Big Knock." *Sports Illustrated*. 19 Aug. 1985.

84. "The strange life and ownership of Chris Von der Ahe." Hetrick, J. Thomas. *Chris Von der Ahe and the St. Louis Browns*. Lanham, MD.: Scarecrow Press, 1999.

84. "Background on Hal Chase as a player." Jones, David. *Deadball Stars of the American League*. Dulles, Va.: Potomac Books, 2006.

84. "The corrupt ways of Hal Chase." Dewey, Donald, Acocella, Nick. *The Black Prince of Baseball: Hal Chase and the Mythology of the Game*. Toronto: SportsClassic Books, 2004.

86. "Life after baseball for Vida Blue." Shea, John. "Tough Pitch." *San Francisco Chronicle*. 5 July 2006.

86. "Vida Blue's amazing 1971 season." Blount, Roy. "Off to a Sizzling Start." *Sports Illustrated*. 31 May 1971.

## CHAPTER 9

89. "Background on Jay Johnstone." Lewis, Allen. "Long Journey to Success." *Baseball Digest*. Dec. 1976.

90. "The life of pitcher Moe Drabowsky." "Prankster pitcher Moe Drabowsky dies at age 70." Associated Press. 12 June 2006.

90. "Moe Drabowsky's antics." Lyon, Bill. "Whatever Happened to All Those Bullpen Pranksters?" *Baseball Digest*. Nov. 1977.

90. "Ryan Dempster on his antics." "Ryan Dempster, the Cubs' Class Clown." Published at theheckler.com. Jan. 2006.

90. "Ryan Dempster pulls a prank." Sullivan, Paul. "Cubs coach Punk'd by Pitchers." *Chicago Tribune*. 18 March 2008.

93. "Mickey Hatcher's connection to the Metrodome." Caple, Jim. "End of The Domed Era in Minnesota." Published at ESPN.com. 3 Oct. 2009.

93. "Mickey Hatcher on the famous Metrodome gag." Hatcher, Mickey. "The Ball That Never Came Down." Published at ESPN.com. 30 Sept. 2009

93. "On pranks by Mickey Hatcher and Jay Johnstone." Lasorda, Tommy. Plaschke, Bill. *I Live For This*. New York: Houghton Mifflin, 2007.

94. "Kevin Millar on the Red Sox's pregame routine." Gammons, Peter. "Millar: 'It wasn't as if guys were drunk.'" Published at ESPN.com. 2 Nov. 2004.

94. "Kevin Millar on his personality." McWilliam, Bryan. "Webchat with Kevin Millar." Published at BlueJays.gearup.com. 9 Sept. 2009.

94. "A video prank on Kevin Millar." Lane, Laura. "Inside MLB Pranks." *ESPN The Magazine*. 26 Aug. 2008.

96. "The pranks of Larry Andersen." Kerby, Ray. "An Interview with Larry Andersen." Published at TheAstroDaily.com. 28 Nov. 2001.

97. "The pranks of Steve Lyons, Larry Andersen." Liebmann, Glenn. "Here Are Some New Names for the Humor Hall of Fame." *Baseball Digest*. March 1992.

97. "Background on Steve Lyons." Joseph, Dave. "Baseball Aches for Flakes." *Baseball Digest*. Aug. 2003.

97. "Reliving Steve Lyons' dropped pants." Swift, E.M. "Moon Man." *Sports Illustrated*. 13 Aug. 1990.

## CHAPTER 10

98. "Background on Jackie Robinson." Schwartz, Larry. "Jackie Changed The Face of Sports." Published at ESPN.com. 2007

98. "Jackie Robinson as a player." Nack, William. "The Breakthrough." *Sports Illustrated*. 5 May 1997.

98. "Jackie Robinson's obituary." Anderson, Dave. "Jackie Robinson, First Black in Major Leagues, Dies." *The New York Times*. 25 Oct. 1972.

100. "The life and career of John Montgomery Ward." Stevens, David. *Baseball's Radical for All Seasons*. Lanham, MD: Scarecrow Press,1998.

101. "History of Rube Foster." Foster, Rube. Negro League Baseball Players Association. 2007.

103. "Looking back at Moe Berg." Davidoff, Nicholas. "Scholar, Lawyer, Catcher, Spy." *Sports Illustrated*. 23 March 1992.

104. "Branch Rickey talks about his life in baseball." Holland, Gerald. "Mr. Rickey and The Game." *Sports Illustrated*. 7 March 1955.

104. "The Life of Branch Rickey." "Branch Rickey, 83, dies in Missouri." United Press International. 10 Dec. 1965.

106. "Roy Campanella in a photo history." Harnisch, Larry. "Roy Campanella pictures." *Los Angeles Times*. 28 Jan. 2008.

106. "The impact of Roy Campanella." Fimrite, Ron. "Baseball's Best Ambassador." *Sports Illustrated*. 5 July 1993.

108. "The fall and rise of Ron LeFlore." Rhoden, William. "Stealing Home." *Ebony*. Oct. 1975.

## CHAPTER 11

110. "Harry Caray's obituary." Sandomir, Richard. "Harry Caray, 78, Colorful Baseball Announcer Dies." *The New York Times*. 19 Feb. 1998.

110. "Harry Caray's Funeral." Bluth, Andrew. "Harry Caray Remembered as Baseball Ambassador." *The New York Times*. 28 Feb. 1998.

112. "Ozzie Guillen on being old school." Van Dyck, Dave. "Chicago's Ozzie Guillen Piles On his Anti-TV rant." *Chicago Tribune*. 28 Sept. 2009.

112. "Ozzie Guillen on Wrigley Field." Cherner, Reid; Weir, Tom. "Wrigley Makes Ozzie Guillen Puke." Published at USAToday.com. 15 June 2009.

112. "Leo Durocher's obituary." Rogers, Thomas. "Leo Durocher, Fiery Ex-Manager, Dies at 86." *The New York Times*. 8 Oct. 1981.

112. "Branch Rickey talks about giving Durocher another chance." Holland, Gerald. "Mr. Rickey and The Game." *Sports Illustrated*. 7 March 1955.

112. "Leo Durocher talks about Willie Mays' catch." Gergen, Joe. "50th Anniversary of Giants World Series." *Newsday*. 29 Sept. 2004.

115. "The Hall of Fame journey for Phil Rizzuto." Povich, Shirley. "As Lefty, Leo enter, Wait Lifted for Scooter." *Washington Post*. 1 Aug. 1994.

115. "Memories of Phil Rizzuto." Buscema, Dave. "Scooter — A Little Man with a Big Heart." *Times Herald-Record of Hudson Valley*. 15 Aug. 2007.

115. "Origins of Phil Rizzuto's nickname." Bernstein, Adam. "Yankees Hall of Famer, Broadcaster Phil Rizzuto." *Washington Post*. 15 Aug. 2007.

116. Bob Uecker enters Hall of Fame." Cushman, Tom. "No hit, just wit." *San Diego Union-Tribune*. 27 July 2003.

116. "Uecker's broadcasting career remembered." Hunt, Michael. "Uecker Brings Special Brand of Humor to Hall of Fame." *Milwaukee Journal Sentinel*. 13 March 2003.

116. "Uecker's broadcasting peak." Walker, Ben. "Uecker Moves to Front Row in Baseball Hall of Fame." Associated Press. 13 March 2003

119. "Ring Lardner's passing." Harrison, Dale. "Ring Lardner, Noted Writer of Humor, Dies of Long Fight Against Tuberculosis." *The Evening Independent*. 26 Sept. 1933.

119. "Life of Jerry Coleman." Kernan, Kevin. "Caster Coleman True Hero, Ex-Yanks 2B was Pilot in World War II, Korea." New York *Post*. 21 Oct. 1998.

119. "Coleman's War stories." "Leitner Silent? In his Dreams." *San Diego Union-Tribune*. 19 June 1998.

119. "Coleman as a broadcaster." Drooz, Alan. "Oh Doctor, You Can Hang A Star On this One." *San Diego Union-Tribune*. 16 Aug. 2001.

121. "Yogi Berra quotes through the years." McKay, Mary Jane. "The Wisdom of the Yogi-isms." Published at CBSnews.com. 9 July 2003.

## CHAPTER 12

122. "The obituary of Max Patkin." Goldstein, Richard. "Max Patkin, 79, Clown Prince of Baseball." *The New York Times*. 1 Nov. 1999.

122. "The acting debut of Max Patkin." Cohn, Al. "People Section." *Newsday*. 17 June 1988.

122. "Funny quote from Max Patkin." "Sound Off." *Eugene Register-Guard*. 31 Aug. 1980.

124. "The obituary of Frenchy Bordagaray." Goldstein, Richard. "Frenchy Bordagaray is Dead; The Colorful Dodger was 90." *The New York Times*. 23 May 2000.

125. "Background on Bo Belinsky." Joseph, Dave. "Baseball Aches for Flakes." *Baseball Digest*. Aug. 2003.

127. "The life of Nick Altrock." "Nick Altrock Still Happy After 42 Years In Sport." Associated Press. 22 Jan. 1939.

127. "The comeback of Al Schacht." "Schacht Announces Comeback; Admits he's Probably Kidding." Associated Press. 13 April 1943.

128. "Tracking down Joe Charboneau in the minors." Zielinksi, Michael. "Where Have You Gone, Joe Charboneau?" *Reading Eagle*. 25 April 1983.

131. "History of Arlie Latham." Berger, Ralph. "Arlie Latham page." The Baseball Biography Project. Published at bioproj.sabr.org.

133. "Background on Germany Schaefer." Jones, David. *Deadball Stars of the American League*. Dulles, Va.: Potomac Books, 2006.

133. "Antics of Germany Schaefer." Jardine, Jeff. "A One-of-A-Kind Baseball Original." *The Modesto Bee*. 27 March 1993.

133. "An Appearance by Jackie Price." Warner, Ralph. "Comedian Jackie Price Shows at Game Tonight." *Miami News*. 1 May 1954.

133. "Public loses interest in Jackie Price." Welsh, Charles. "Jackie Price Finding Fewer Places to Show." Associated Press. 11 Aug. 1959.

## CHAPTER 13

134. "The exploits of Kirby Puckett." Berkow, Ira. "Kirby Puckett is a Rich Man." *The New York Times*. 14 Oct. 1991

134. "The obituary of Kirby Puckkett." Bodley, Hal. "Hall of Famer Kirby Puckett Dies after Massive Stroke." *USA Today*. 6 March 2006.

136. "Tug McGraw's antics." Lyon, Bill. "Whatever Happened to All Those Bullpen Pranksters?" *Baseball Digest*. Nov. 1977.

136. "The obituary of Tug McGraw." Litzky, Frank. "Tug McGraw, 59, Is Dead; Star with Mets and Phillies." *The New York Times*. 6 Jan. 2004.

136. "The memories of Tug McGraw." Mandel, Ken. "Tug McGraw dies at 59." Published at MLB.com. 5 Jan. 2004.

138. "The obituary of Willie Stargell." Goldstein, Richard. "A Force for the Pirates at Bat and in the Clubhouse, Dies at 61." *The New York Times*. 10 April 2001.

138. "Willie Stargell as a Leader." Musick, Phil. "Willie the Leader." *Pittsburgh Press*. 4 June 1973.

139. "Minnie joins the Cardinals." "Minnie Minoso Bringing Life Into Cardinal Camp." Associated Press. 30 March 1962.

140. "Dontrelle Willis relates to a veteran." O'Connor, Ian. "Unique Bond Lifts Rookie Willis." *USA Today*. 29 June 2003.

140. "Pitching coach on Willis' delivery." Chen, Albert. "Big Fish." *Sports Illustrated*. 9 May 2005.

140. "Willis talks about anxiety disorder." Latsch, Nate. "Willis Back On DL with Anxiety Disorder." Published at MLB.com. 18 June 2009.

142. "Life on the bench for Chico Ruiz." Murray, Jim. "Ruiz Is Champ Bench Warmer." *The Modesto Bee*. 20 May 1970.

143. "The passing of Buck O'Neil." Conroy, Scott. "Baseball Great Buck O'Neil passes at 94." Published at CBSnews.com. 6 Oct. 2006.

143. "Memories of Buck O'Neil." "Former Negro Leaguer O'Neil Dies." Associated Press. 18 Oct. 2006.

145. "The obituary of Joe Black." Goldstein, Richard. "Joe Black, Pitching Pioneer for The Dodgers, Dies at 78." *The New York Times*. 18 May 2002.

145. "Joe Black on starting a World Series game." "Joe Black Says Yankees 'Don't Awe Me at All.'" Associated Press. 1 Oct. 1952.

## CHAPTER 14

146. "Reggie Jackson on his majestic home runs." Jr. Blount, Ron. "Everyone is Helpless and In Awe." *Sports Illustrated*. 17 June 1974.

149. "The $10,000 sale of the Diamond Beauty, King Kelly." "A New Brotherhood Man." *The New York Times*. 25 Nov. 1889.

150. "Deion Sanders talks about focusing on baseball." Hinton, Ed. "One Thing or The Other." *Sports Illustrated*. 27 April 1992.

150. "Yankees tire of Deion Sanders' distraction." Curry, Jack. "Deion Sanders Placed on Waivers By Yanks." *The New York Times*. 25 Sept. 1990.

150. "Prime Time takes on Pudge." Crasnick, Jerry. "On-field Antics That Have Struck A Chord." Published at ESPN.com. 14 May 2008.

150. "Sanders on his return to baseball." Kay, Joe. "Sanders Goes 3-for-3 in his Reds' Re-debut." Associated Press. 1 May 2001.

152. "Bo Jackson thinking about the NFL." "Bo's New Hobby: Football." Associated Press. 12 July 1987.

152. "Bo Jackson on life in the NFL." "Jackson Proves He's at Home in the NFL." Associated Press. 2 Dec. 1987.

152. "Bo Jackson on playing two sports." Rhoden, William. "Bo Jackson: Baseball In the Long Run." *The New York Times*. 13 Dec. 1987.

152. "Bo Jackson on his hip injury." Chass, Murray. "White Sox Decide To Gamble on Bo Jackson." *The New York Times*. 4 April 1991.

154. "Babe Ruth's legacy." Quinn, T.J. "Bambino Remains Larger Than Life." New York *Daily News*. 15 July 2003.

154. "Babe Ruth's passing." "Nation Mourns for Ruth, Nation's Greatest Baseball Hero." *Miami Daily News*. 17 Aug. 1948.

# CREDITS

# INDEX